D1623878

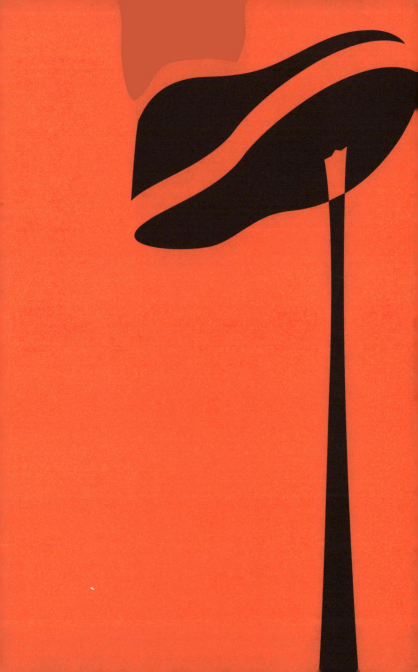

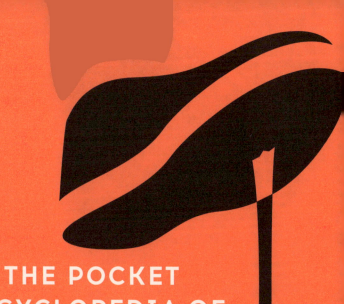

THE POCKET
ENCYCLOPEDIA OF
AGGRAVATION

THE POCKET ENCYCLOPEDIA OF AGGRAVATION

97 Things That Annoy, Bother, Chafe, Disturb, Enervate, Frustrate, Grate, Harass, Irk, Jar, Miff, Nettle, Outrage, Peeve, Quassh, Rile, Stress Out, Trouble, Upset, Vex, Worry, and X Y Z You!

LAURA LEE
Illustrated by LINDA O'LEARY

BLACK DOG
& LEVENTHAL
PUBLISHERS
NEW YORK

081
Lee

10/17
B+

Black Dog & Leventhal Publishers
Hachette Book Group
1290 Avenue of the Americas
New York, NY 10104

www.hachettebookgroup.com
www.blackdogandleventhal.com

Originally published in hardcover: September 2001

First Revised Edition: September 2017

Black Dog & Leventhal Publishers is an imprint of Hachette Books, a division of Hachette Book Group. The Black Dog & Leventhal Publishers name and logo are trademarks of Hachette Book Group, Inc.

The publisher is not responsible for websites (or their content) that are not owned by the publisher.

The Hachette Speakers Bureau provides a wide range of authors for speaking events. To find out more, go to www.HachetteSpeakersBureau.com or call (866) 376-6591.

Print book interior design by Red Herring Design.

Library of Congress Cataloging-in-Publication Data has been applied for.

LSC-C

ISBNs: 978-0-316-47195-4 (paper over board) 978-0-316-47346-0 (ebook)

Printed in the United States of America

10 9 8 7 6 5 4 3 2 1

CONTENTS

*"I said to myself, Arlo, if you were dead,
a lot of the stuff that pisses you off
probably wouldn't bother you so much."*

—ARLO GUTHRIE, introduction to the song "Wake up Dead"

INTRODUCTION

I t has been more than fifteen years since that August afternoon when the idea for a book bit me on the leg. I was sitting beside a pond, lazily contemplating the way the sun reflected off the ripples in the water, when my reveries were interrupted by the itchy poke of a mosquito boring into me with her sipper. My mind was filled with questions. Why do mosquitoes flock to me more than to other people? What makes that lump appear on the skin? What makes it itch? Why are there annoying things like mosquitoes on the planet, anyway? It occurred to me that other people must wonder about this kind of thing as well. Why do I keep losing socks in the wash? Why am I always in the slowest line at the supermarket? Is there a correct answer when the cop asks, "Do you know how fast you were going?" I did not know, at that moment, that I was about to write my most successful book, and that eighteen or so books later, I would never surpass it in sales. (Annoying!) Who knew that pet peeves could be so profitable? It seems there is something gratifying in the realization that other people have been bugged by these little occurrences and even more gratifying to know why they happen. (Not as gratifying as if they did not happen in the first place, mind you, but gratifying nonetheless.) People are frustrated by thousands of little things, from hangnails and paper cuts to the mother of all aggravations— telemarketers, who are, incidentally, making a comeback. When the futurists of days gone by imagined a brave new world full of robots, they never dreamed these advances in technology would be used to call you in the middle of dinner to sell prescription drugs. It seems nearly every step in the march of human progress lands in dog doo.

No one is immune. On several occasions, the experts I consulted—scientists with long titles and multiple PhDs—ended our conversation by ranting about those little threads that hang from sweaters, people chewing on pencils, and fitted sheets that don't.

For example, I contacted Dr. Ron Grassi, D.C., M.S., DABDA, FACFE, Diplomate American Boards of Forensic Medical Examiners & Physical Disability Analysts, with a question about why stiff necks hurt so much. (An entry which, incidentally, did not make the final cut. Sorry about that.) Along with my answer I got the following: "Why do people scream on cell phones like they're yelling across a canyon? They don't do this on a regular phone. How about someone scraping the ice cream bowl with a spoon (after there is hardly any left) while you're lying in bed at night watching a movie. And the DOOR SLAMMERS!!!!! Do you know how insulting that is to a Corvette convertible?" Other experts were not as amused by the concept. A representative of Rensselaer Polytechnic Institute seemed a bit annoyed when I phoned to ask if there was a mechanical engineer who could explain why a handheld can opener slides off the rim, leaving that little bit of joined metal that you can't seem to cut through when you start with the opener again. (I never did get an answer to that one.) One local librarian was confused when I came in and explained that I was looking for the psychology books because I wanted to find out why two pedestrians trying to get out of each other's way both dodge in the same direction, then both dodge to the opposite side, and end up doing an odd sidewalk dance. "You're not going to find any books on that," she said with a squint that clearly indicated she was sure I was insane or making fun of her or both. In my original introduction, I wrote that we should be optimistic about the fact that Americans are obsessed with the dust on their computer monitors and legroom on airplanes. You can only muster the energy to get upset about these things when the outer world is in a state of relative peace, tranquility, and prosperity. Although I have not found statistics to back it up, my guess is that scientists spend much less time and energy trying to figure out the exact chemical composition of intestinal gas or how long it takes a cookie to turn to mush in your mug when the nation is in the midst of war, famine, plague, or economic depression. In the absence of a huge national crisis, we have the freedom to ponder the little things. In that spirit, this is a highly uplifting work. That's what I wrote just before my book came out—the week of September 11, 2001. Given my reasonable hypothesis, I was sure *The Pocket Encyclopedia of Aggravation* was destined to disappear without a trace. But we returned to life and laughter and, importantly for me, complaining about the little things that get on our nerves. There is no escape from aggravation. People who live and work in cities deal with smog, long lines, traffic jams, noise, crowds, and a more fidgety, tension-filled lifestyle. People who live in the country have their own annoyances: bugs, roadkill, stepping in cow dung, and having to drive 20 minutes to get to the nearest post office. Some people choose to work in offices, where they deal with difficult coworkers and bosses, uninspiring environments of office cubicles, and having to plan months in advance to get days off. Others avoid those hassles by being self-employed. They deal with self-employment tax, paying for medical insurance out of pocket, and not having a weekly paycheck. People who live alone have to pay all the rent and there's no one at the house to call for help if the car breaks down. People who live together have to compromise more. I have come to the conclusion that the key to life is choosing which annoyances you prefer to deal with and adjusting your lifestyle accordingly.

Annoyances are subjective, I know. I once worked as a mime. One person's noise is another's symphony. One's aromatherapy is another's loud perfume. I compiled my original list of annoying things from personal observation and suggestions from friends and acquaintances. If I had written entries for all the items on my master list, it would rival the *Oxford English Dictionary* for shelf space. For some reason, my publisher thought that might make it hard to sell. I reduced the list by focusing on the aggravations that seem to elicit the most venom, and those that have the most interesting explanations. Over time, however, *The Pocket Encyclopedia* had become a bit stale. In the intervening years, the word "cyber" went from futuristic to old fashioned; they decided to take the hyphen out of the word email; and the jury is still out on whether or not to capitalize Internet. We managed to make it through an entire decade without ever coming to a consensus about what to call it. The zeroes? The 2000s? The aughts? CDs skipping, the laser pointer fad, and VCR clocks that flash 12:00 because you can't figure out how to set them lost their power to drive us nuts. A recent study concluded that men no longer hog the television remote control. We have reached a golden age of remote control parity . . . just as we are starting to watch videos on devices other than televisions. Beginning in 2009, a new law reduced the number of hidden fees and penalties that credit card companies can charge. The amount of luggage that gets misrouted by airlines has been significantly reduced thanks to better computer tracking systems. There were even aggravations that came and went before I could document them. For example, the iPhone was introduced and it came with pre-installed apps you were not allowed to delete. So you had to put them in their own special folder called "Apple Junk" that you hid on the fifth screen. (I'm talking to you "Stocks!") This year, Apple finally decided to let you delete them and a decade from now no one will remember they ever annoyed you in that way. I have confidence, however, that they will find new ways. (This is, after all, the company that removed the headphone jack and sold you an expensive dongle to replace it, calling it a brave innovation.) On a personal note, since the last edition of this book, I've come to know the frustration of having your reading glasses always in the other room. You see, botheration is a constant. The saccharine purple dinosaur we loved to hate in the 1990s was replaced with Pokémon Go. Cassette tapes that unwind and get eaten by the machine and video rental late fees may be things of the past, but they were replaced with buffering delays, selfie sticks, and a whole host of social-networking woes. Ten years from now, there will be something new, wondrous, consequential, and full of unforeseen side effects. Before we get to the main event, I want to take a moment to address one of the frequent·complaints of grammar purists who gripe about such things in their blogs. There are those who feel that "aggravation" is the wrong word to describe life's little frustrations. Aggravation, they say, is *making something worse.* Indeed, this is the first definition of the word. Using aggravation to mean irritation or annoyance is, however, an accepted usage. If you don't think it ought to be, you've been outvoted by the people who write dictionaries. So there! For some reason, I'm not as much on board with dictionary authors' decision in 2013 to include the popular use of the word "literally" to mean not something that is actually true but literally its opposite. (As in "My head literally exploded.") On the subject of linguistic annoyances, one thing that has not changed since the first edition is that an inordinate number of vexations seem to start with the letter "C" and I still couldn't think of anything annoying that starts with Q. What are you going to do?

Brain processing complicated concepts

Unintelligible prose

ACADEMIC LANGUAGE

"Since thought is seen to be 'rhizomatic' rather than 'arboreal,' the movement of differentiation and becoming is already imbued with its own positive trajectory," is from *The Continental Philosophy Reader*, edited by Richard Kearney and Mara Rainwater. The line is part of an introduction intended to help students understand the chapter. Sure. That explains it.

Why do academics insist on writing in language that makes the reader squint and develop a headache? It is simply a matter of style, say defenders of dense, challenging prose. Different forums have different rules. *People* magazine has a different style from the *New York Times*, which has a different style than the Sears catalog. Every profession has its jargon. Academic specialties have more than their share because they are expressing complicated and often new ideas.

"There's a kind of presumption among journalists and people

who talk about culture in the media that if it's written by an English professor, it should be comprehensible to others," Dr. Eric Mallin, an associate professor in the English Department at the University of Texas at Austin, told the *Dallas Morning News*. "That's assuming there is no specialized knowledge particular to the field."

Dr. Judith Butler, professor at the University of California at Berkeley, was unwittingly thrust into the center of the academic writing debate when the New Zealand publication *Philosophy and Literature* awarded a ninety-word sample of one of her articles the top prize in its annual Bad Writing Contest. The "honor" is given to the most "stylistically awful sentence" to come out of the scholarly world.

Butler defended her style of writing in a *New York Times* op-ed piece. Academic writing needs to be "difficult and demanding," she said, in order to question concepts that are so ingrained no one thinks to question them. Having to think about the meaning of each sentence provokes new ways of looking at a familiar world.

Others believe the jargon has little to do with communication. They see it as something akin to a secret handshake or a series of multisyllabic passwords. It is written to confirm academic authority, membership in the club.

In 1996, a New York University physicist submitted an article with fake phrases and gibberish to the journal *Social Text*, which published it as genuine scholarly analysis. When an English professor at Southern Oregon University was asked to paraphrase a long sentence from the Bad Writing Contest's second prize winner, he admitted, "It doesn't make a lot of sense to me."

Yet to gain tenure, professors must publish, and to be published, they must adopt the accepted style. Philosopher Bertrand Russell summed it up in his essay "How I Write." "I am allowed to use plain English because everybody knows that I could use mathematical logic if I chose," he wrote. "I suggest to young professors that their first work should be written in a jargon only to be understood by the erudite few. With that behind them, they can ever after say what they have to say in a language 'understanded of the people.'"

ACNE

When you reach that special age when you start to think about trying to attract a boyfriend or girlfriend, you become preoccupied with your appearance— and then Mother Nature reveals she has a sick sense of humor. Your skin begins to change, an oily sheen covers your face and pimples pop up everywhere. What is more, the stress of having acne can give you acne!

The tendency to get acne is inherited. Males are more prone to it than females during their teenage years, but because it is hormonally triggered, adult women often have outbreaks of acne that correspond with their menstrual cycles. Scientists speculate that this side effect of puberty once had a purpose. In the days when people hunted and foraged for food in the wild, the skin may have needed extra protection from the elements as we reached adulthood. Now the overactive oil glands just give you zits.

Androgens, the sex hormones released at puberty, cause the production of sebum, the fat that naturally keeps your skin and hair soft. Somehow, though, the sebum gets trapped along with dead skin cells. The follicle stretches outward and a bump forms on top. Contrary to popular belief, blackheads are not caused by dirt that gets stuck in a pore. Blackheads are oil plugs that make their way to the surface and turn dark when the air hits them. If they are covered and can't break through the surface, the oil plug stays white.

When the sebum in the blocked gland is transformed into free fatty acids they become food for bacteria. The body responds by sending white blood cells to kill the intruders. The result is pus and a big pimple.

The tendency to get acne couldn't come at a worse time in life. David Elkind, who studied egocentrism in adolescence, showed that during our teen years we become preoccupied with our self-image. We feel there is an imaginary audience watching our every move—an audience full of critics. Stress—having a big test, a job interview, a big date, or an outbreak of acne at a time when you feel especially self-conscious—causes your body to release more androgens, which can trigger new pimple outbreaks, which can cause more stress, which causes your body to release more androgens and so on, and so on.

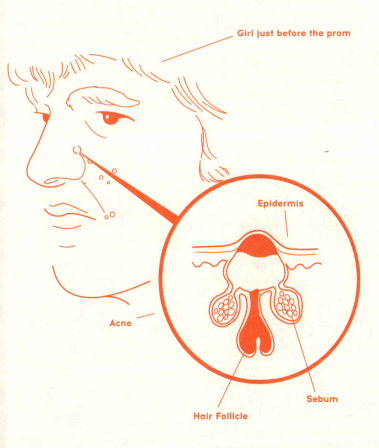

Girl just before the prom

Epidermis

Acne

Sebum

Hair Follicle

Seatback
fully
reclined

AIRPLANE LEGROOM, OR THE SEATBACK IN YOUR FACE . . .

ou're in the middle seat. Your bag is stowed under the seat in front of you, which means you can't stretch your feet out in front of you—unless you call putting your tootsies a couple of inches forward "stretching." Your neighbors have taken both armrests and now the guy in the seat in front of you decides to lean his seat all the way back. Your thimble-sized cup of coffee is now on your lap, and you have about as much freedom of movement as a body in a coffin.

Travel, for those of us back in the steerage class, is uncomfortable and psychologically stressful because other people are planted well within our bounds of personal space. "Quite frankly, I don't think this issue would even exist if we passed a law that required all executives of the nation's airlines to fly in the middle seat on coach," said former Alaska Senator Frank Murkowski.

The FAA does have regulations as to the configuration of the seats. They must be designed to insure that all passengers can exit an aircraft in an emergency within a specified period of time. There are no regulations that assure minimum comfort. To make matters worse, airlines are fuller than they've ever been. Throughout most of the twentieth century they flew with loads of 50 to 60 percent. Ten years ago load capacity rose to 70 percent. Now it is 84 percent. And the airlines keep inventing new ways to shoehorn us in.

Until the 1980s, the distance between your seat back and the one in front of you was 34 inches. When the first edition of this book came out in 2001, I reported that carriers had cut that down to 31 or 32 inches. Today airlines routinely provide between 28 and 31 inches. As travel writer Scott McCartney put it, "one passenger's nose may be three inches closer to the back of the head in front of her." Some psychologists believe what's going on at eye level stresses us out more than any lack of leg room.

That is not to say the other parts of your anatomy are comfortable in an airline seat. According to Kathleen Robinette, who studies body measurements for the U.S. Air Force, the design of the seats has always been faulty. Sometime back in the 1960s, designers opted to base the width of the seat on the average dimension of male hips. They assumed, as men are larger than women, that a seat that fit a man would fit a woman as well. There are two problems with this. First, the shoulders and arms are wider than the hips, so fitting your backside does not prevent you from rubbing against your neighbor or spilling out into the aisle. Second, women's hips are wider than men's. So seats never quite worked for everyone to begin with. The result, Robinette says, is that the seats were about five inches too narrow in the 1960s. In the 1970s and 80s, average seats were between 18 and 20 inches. These days they are 16.5 to 17.5 inches even though the average American gained 30 pounds and increased his hip size to 20.6 inches in the same time period. So bigger passengers, smaller seats. But here's the thing: as much as we love to complain about the lack of legroom, unpalatable airline food, and having to pay for movie headsets (come on, I paid $400 for this ticket and you can't give me a headset for free?), we want our travel to be cheap. We buy airline tickets by going online and seeking out the lowest price. If the booking sites provided an option to search by legroom and other amenities, perhaps we would shop that way. This would make sense in the new world of à la carte pricing, but so far none of them do. Until that changes, to get our economy class business, airlines are in a race to the bottom to offer the cheapest ticket. You can, however, do a bit of research on your own using a site like SeatGuru.com which shows the specific jet and the configuration in each section.

ALUMINUM FOIL AGAINST DENTAL FILLINGS

You sit down to lunch at the office and carefully unwrap a ham sandwich from a sheet of aluminum foil. Unbeknownst to you, a small piece has remained in the sandwich and when you bite into your lunch the foil is pressed between your fillings. A sharp pain vibrates through your teeth, as if a sadistic dentist were trying to inspire a Pavlovian fear of ham on white. The pain is literally an electric shock.

This happens when you have traditional dental fillings made of mercury combined with either tin or silver. The aluminum foil acts as an anode, the filling as a cathode and your saliva is an electrolyte "salt bridge." The result is a galvanic cell, which releases an electrical current of up to two volts. Believe it or not, at least one researcher says chewing on tinfoil is good for you. According to the Wireless Flash News Service, researcher Miklos Gombkoto of the Hungarian Dental University of Gyor did a month-long study in which twenty, presumably broke, Hungarian college students agreed to chew aluminum foil for thirty seconds, three times a day, for $75. Gombkoto reported that the electrical charge helped kill germs in the mouth that cause bad breath and tooth decay. Feel free to experiment on your own.

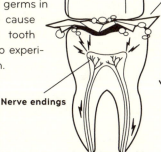

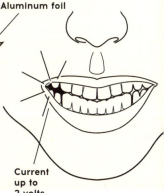

Aluminum foil

Nerve endings

Current up to 2 volts

ANNOYING COMMERCIALS, OR "YOU'VE GOT RING AROUND THE COLLAR!"

See also *Pop-Up Ads.*

"Can you hear me now?" "I've fallen, and I can't get up!" "Guess what day it is? Hump day!" "It slices, it dices, it juliennes, call in the next half hour and get an extra knife absolutely free! Now how much would you pay?"

They shout at you, cajole you. They have grating voices, inane catch phrases, animated walking, overactive bladders, frolicking foot fungus, and lists of possible side effects including rash, sleepwalking, and death. There are people who are way too excited about discount apps and sales on office supplies, and others who nag you about things like ring around the collar, knocks and pings, blackheads, and that little itch that could be telling them you have dandruff. You already have a mother, thank you very much.

You'd think advertisers would do everything in their power to get on your good side. Not so. Advertisers today have quite a task to get your attention. Every day the average American is bombarded with 360 advertising messages per day across all media. When you add brand impressions—things like a logo on a t-shirt or bag—it jumps up to 5,000. Of those, only 100 or so make any kind of impression at all. You entirely forget having seen the rest. This is a problem for marketers. If they can't get your attention, they fail. In the same way that stepping on a piece of glass is more memorable than stepping on a feather, a commercial that insults your intelligence, rattles your ears, or otherwise annoys you is more likely to be remembered.

Some of the finest examples of the annoying genre came out of the 1970s when our attention spans were just starting to get really taxed. That's when Ron Popeil came on the scene. His Ronco direct television spots were made with a shoestring budget. Popeil wanted to use every second of his $7.50-a-minute time so he spoke as fast as he could, edited out pauses for breath and sped the whole thing up mechanically. The hyper-pitch sold Veg-O-Matics, Mr. Dentist, the Pocket Fisherman, and Mr. Microphone "Hey baby, I'll be back to pick you up later!" The commercials presented a problem and an "as seen on TV" product that was the solution.

"Play this game with yourself," Popeil told the *Palm Beach Post*. "Pick any object on your desk. First, come up with a scenario of all the problems that product solves. Then introduce the product. Then show how the product works. Then tell the customer how to buy the product. Do that in 30 seconds' time, and it sounds like someone's trying to shove this thing down your throat."

Another company, Dial Media, followed in Ronco's footsteps. They took a knife and gave it the Japanese-sounding name Ginsu. To the hyper hard sell they added a new twist, freebies. Buy a Ginsu knife and you get a cleaver, a bread knife, table knives—but wait, there's more!—a set of spoons. These folks were the forerunners. They blazed a trail for today's infomercials and home shopping networks. Let's face it, if they weren't presented to you on late night TV would you ever think you needed a Chia Pet, the Clapper, spray-on hair, or a singing robot fish? Now how much would you pay?

A

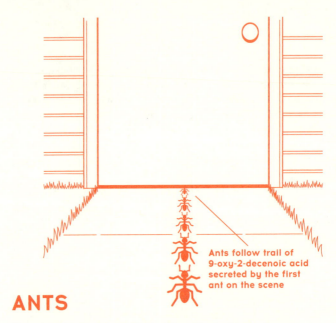

Ants follow trail of 9-oxy-2-decenoic acid secreted by the first ant on the scene

ANTS

See also *Cockroaches, Fleas, Flies, Gnats, Mosquitoes*.

Ah spring. The flowers grow once more, the sun shines . . . and your kitchen is suddenly swarming with ants. They're everywhere, and they just keep coming.

Why do ants suddenly appear in such large numbers in spring? Over the winter, ants stay in their underground nests. They subsist on the stores of food they collected over the summer. When it gets warm, the population swells and the workers head out once again to collect nourishment. A crumb that is barely noticeable to a human is a tasty feast for an ant.

According to the trade magazine *Pest Control*, homeowners now rank ants ahead of cockroaches as their biggest insect headache. It's good news for the pest control business. They call ants the industry's most "economically important pest." Still, ant control seems to be "starting from ground zero," Dr. William Robinson, president of Urban Pest Ants reported.

Most of the ants you see indoors are female workers who live in colonies outdoors. If you observe them for long, you will see that they are marching to and from a food source and carrying nourishment out of your home back to the queen. When a worker ant comes across food, she starts secreting pheremones from an abdominal gland. Other ants follow the scent and reinforce it with their own trails. As the food is exhausted, the ants stop secreting and the trail dries up. They are so guided by the scent that if you were to wipe your finger across it and create a break in the path, the ants traveling in both directions would come to a complete stop.

Poisonous sprays are strangely satisfying, but they don't work in the long run. You get to see a few worker ants fall on their backs and die, but the poison never makes it back to the queen. As soon as their friends find the way back, you'll see ants again.

There are other reasons to avoid sprays. As many as 500 species of the most common household insects are now resistant to many of the most widely used insecticides according to Sheila Daar, executive director of the Bio-Integral Resource Center in Berkley, California. They can still be dangerous to humans, especially children.

Ant traps work by offering a supply of poisoned food in a dosage small enough to make it back to the nest. If the baits are too strong and you see dead ants around it, leave them where they are; eventually, other ants will take their corpses back to the nest where they will poison the colony. Dead ants have their own pheromone, 10-octadecenoic acid. Ants treat a dead peer as if it were living until they smell the acid. Then they take the body to the dead ant dumping ground. If you put the acid on a living ant, the other ants will pick it up and dump it as well. The discarded ant will return only to be carried off again until the acid evaporates.

Instead of spraying, see if you can figure out where the ants are coming from. You can block the entry with a glob of petroleum jelly or toothpaste. Then clean up their path with soapy water. This will eliminate the chemical trails the scouts left for other workers.

ARMREST WARS

See also *Inefficient Sidewalk Pass, Standing Too Close.*

Y ou're next to a big man on a long airplane journey. The insensitive, space-hogging guy has his oversized limb on the armrest. This is completely rude and unfair because you want the armrest to yourself. Without making eye contact, you wedge your elbow behind his. With each bump, you try to jostle your arm a little bit further forward, but his arm has become as stiff as a board. No way is he giving up. His muscles may cramp up, but his hairy forearm is going to be on that armrest until someone pries it off.

Psychologists call the areas of disputed personal space "ambivalent zones." Whether or not you get into a confrontation depends on who is in the adjoining seat. Our bubble of personal space expands or contracts depending on how we feel about the other person. If it's a friend, family member, or someone you're attracted to, you probably won't have a problem.

When it is a stranger, the battle lines are drawn. We rarely come to blows over the invasion, or even discuss it. We just reposition ourselves and try to slide our arm into the space. This is because we react to personal space violations by trying not to acknowledge the invader as a person.

When you ask ethics experts, as an enterprising reporter at the *Wall Street Journal* did in 2011, they were largely in agreement that the person in the middle seat deserves both armrests in compensation. The unofficial rule is: middle seats, two arm rests; aisle seat, outside armrest; window seat, armrest near the wall.

This is how we generally agree it is supposed to work. It is not what we do. If the research done on this in the 1980s still holds (it doesn't appear that there has been a more recent follow up), when a man sits beside a woman, odds are five-to-one that he'll take the armrest. Dorothy M. Hai and her team from the St. Bonaventure

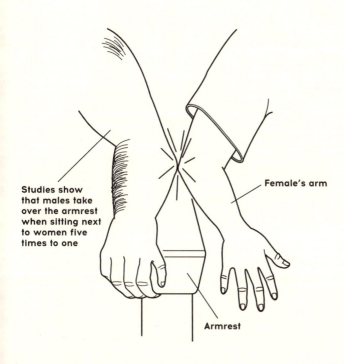

Studies show that males take over the armrest when sitting next to women five times to one

Female's arm

Armrest

University School of Business observed men and women on commercial airline flights and found that a man takes up more space regardless of whether he is bigger or smaller than the woman.

The researchers followed up by interviewing about one hundred of their subjects. They learned that travelers were fully conscious of the elbow war, even if they behaved as if they weren't.

Perhaps we should be grateful, ladies. In 2014 Auburn University microbiologists James Barbaree and Kiril Vaglenov removed materials used in airplanes, put them in environments that mimic flight conditions and found that deadly germs can last for up to a week on the armrest. So go ahead and let him have it.

BAD BREATH ▶ BUREAUCRACY

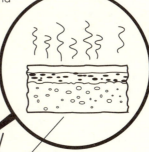

BAD BREATH

See also *Aluminum Foil Against Dental Fillings.*

Breath test: Do people recoil when you exhale? Have you bought stock in Listerine? Do you spend more than 10 percent of your income on mints? Does the dog run away? Has your breath killed small houseplants? You could be one of the estimated 25 to 85 million Americans plagued by bad breath, also known as halitosis or "foetor oris."

"Bad Breath is a problem that originates in the mouth," Dr. Jon Richter told *Men's Health* magazine. It seems obvious enough, but lately a slew of television ads have promoted pills that supposedly fix your breath problem from the inside out. They don't work. Ditto the $1 billion a year we spend on mouthwashes, breath mints, sprays, and gums. Those will reduce the odor for an hour at best.

You probably don't like to think about it, but your mouth has an ecosystem all its own. To a microorganism, your mouth's 95°F temperature and high humidity is like a Hawaiian paradise. More than 400 different species call it home. You feed

Bacteria coating on tongue ferments protein that releases the foul smelling hydrogen sulfide

With high humidity and a temperature of 95 degrees, the mouth is the perfect climate for microorganisms

them every day when you feed yourself. Some of the sugar and carbohydrates stay behind providing a bacterial feast.

The tongues of some people become coated with bacteria that ferment proteins. The fermentation process produces methyl-mercaptan, fatty acids, ammonia, and hydrogen sulfide. This last gas is responsible for the sulfur odor of bad breath. (A similar fermentation process takes place in the intestines: see *Farts*).

No matter how much you brush and floss, your morning mouth probably smells more of sulfur than spearmint. Overnight the micro-organisms that inhabit your mouth have several hours to eat and break down food into amino acids and peptides with their stinky byproducts unmolested by a toothbrush.

Even if you refrained from brushing for the same number of hours during the day, your breath would not smell like it does in the morning. During the day you talk, chew, and swallow. These activities help keep the saliva flowing.

Saliva, it turns out, is pretty amazing stuff. It keeps the ecosystem in your mouth in balance. It contains bicarbonate ions that buffer the tooth-decaying acids produced by bacteria like S. mutans. It also contains phosphate and calcium ions, which repair microscopic cavities. It is full of antibacterial agents and proteins that cause bacteria to stick to each other so they can't stick to the surface of the tooth. The saliva then washes the bacterial clumps away.

During the night, saliva production drops off and its antibacterial action stops as well. The organisms multiply, coat your tongue, and wait for you to get up and grab your toothbrush.

If you seem to have foul breath no matter how much you brush, you probably have what dentists call a "geographic tongue." This means your tongue has more indentations than other people's. This gives anaerobic bacteria extra places in which to live and multiply.

The best way to keep your breath fresh is to clean the back of your tongue. You don't need to buy a fancy tongue cleaner—use an inverted spoon to gently scrape the back of the tongue then rinse.

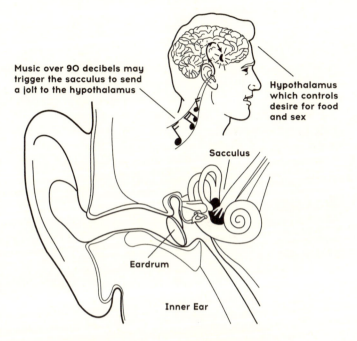

Music over 90 decibels may trigger the sacculus to send a jolt to the hypothalamus

Hypothalamus which controls desire for food and sex

Sacculus

Eardrum

Inner Ear

BOOMING CAR STEREOS, OR THIS IS YOUR BRAIN ON NOISE, ANY QUESTIONS?

See also *Off-Key Singing.*

oom, Boom, Boom, Boom . . . I'm trying to sleep here! Boom, BOOM, BOOM, Boom . . . Your teenage son's car has been fitted with supermega-mondo-killer-ultimate-platinum bass speakers. When they're cranked up which they always are—the car shakes, glass breaks, dogs howl, and small animals run for cover. Your son just bops his multiple-pierced head in appreciation.

Boom-cars are primarily a male obsession. The most devoted enthusiasts of booming music spend thousands of dollars on their audio systems and enter their souped up cars in competitions. The loudest car stereo competition winners of the past few years have blasted in at 155 to 160 decibels, more than twice as loud as a jet taking off and definitely loud enough to cause permanent hearing damage. It only takes about 115 decibels to do that. Emergency sirens, at 120 decibels, don't stand a chance against the loudest boomers.

Robert Franner, editor of the Toronto-based audio trade publication *Marketnews*, once compared sound level competitions to "comparing genitals. It's overkill for people with naturally occurring high levels of testosterone."

Franner may not be too far off. Young males use their booming cars to draw attention, mark territory, and to draw the attention of females. Recent research shows that a boom car is something of a sexual stimulant on wheels. A 2000 study by England's Manchester University found that loud music stimulates a part of the ear that is connected to the brain's pleasure center.

The sacculus, a tiny organ in the inner ear, is part of the system that controls the sense of balance. It does not appear to serve any function in hearing, but it does send messages to the hypothalamus, which controls the human appetite for food and sex. The sacculus is sensitive to sounds over 90 decibels, which may send a kind of pleasure jolt to the brain.

"The distribution of frequencies that are typical in rock concerts and at dance clubs almost seem designed to stimulate the sacculus," Neil Todd, who led the research team, told *New Scientist*. "They are absolutely smack bang in this range of sensitivity."

The pleasure may be addictive. Researchers at Northeastern University in Boston identified what they call Maladaptive Music Listening. People who suffer from MML can't seem to stop listening to loud music even when it is literally deafening. Deprived of a daily loud music blast, the subjects suffered withdrawal symptoms including depression, moodiness, and lethargy. Music over 90 decibels may trigger the sacculus to send a jolt to the hypothalamus.

BUFFERING

See also *Too Many Streaming Services.*

You've invited your best friends over to your house to binge watch the new season of *House of Cards*. The popcorn is popped, you've navigated to your streaming service, and you push play. After five minutes the picture freezes, the dreaded loading thermometer appears on the screen, and you wait, and wait . . .

We love to stream. Six billion hours of YouTube are streamed every month. That is billion with a b. Netflix subscribers alone streamed 42.5 billion hours of programming in 2015. Being able to stream just about any program at any time is one of the joys of the modern age. Having the programs freeze and stop is one of the pains.

B

When a video streams, it's playing as it downloads rather than being downloaded completely before playing on a local machine.

Buffering is when a certain amount of data is downloaded before playback begins so that you do not watch faster than you download. When your streaming gets ahead of the downloading, you experience an interrupt. The larger the size of your buffer, the less likely the playback is to be interrupted. When it works well, buffering is a good thing. But we usually encounter the word "buffering" when things are not working well.

A 2016 study sponsored by the mobile telephone company Ericsson monitored people's brain activity, eye movements, and pulse while doing different everyday smartphone tasks. What did they learn? Slow-loading web pages, buffering, and interrupted videos stress us out. Users' heart rates increased an average of 38 percent when content was delayed. Their stress level was "similar to that of watching a horror movie or solving a mathematical problem and greater than waiting in a checkout line at the grocery store," the report said.

If you're having trouble getting that cat video on YouTube to play properly, there are a few things you can try. First off, make sure you're not running a bunch of programs or apps on your device. Streaming a video takes memory. So closing those programs can help. If the service allows it, pressing pause and letting more of the video download before playback can help. Or start over from the beginning. With any luck, by the time you get back to the part of the film where it got hung up more data will have downloaded and you can proceed normally. If none of this works, you might try logging on at another time. According to the FCC, most streaming occurs between 7 and 11 P.M. When servers get more demand than they can handle, everything slows down. Your experience will probably be better at 3 A.M. Of course, getting up in the middle of the night to watch a movie is also a little bit annoying.

Incidentally, there are two kinds of symbols that show up when digital content is downloading. The throbber is the spinner that lets you know something is happening, but not how long it will take. Then there's a progress bar that appears to tell you how much progress you've made, but actually lies to you. Most of the time, says *Popular Mechanics*, a progress bar that says 50 percent complete could be half done, or it could be just starting. Estimating how long it will take to download or install something is complicated. Most app developers don't really try. They use an off-the-rack code to give a broad ballpark estimate. They are, however, trying to come up with ways to make it seem faster.

Chris Harrison, a PhD candidate at Carnegie Mellon University, tested a variety of animations to come up with the most pleasing tracker. It speeds up as it progresses, and contains a ripple animation that moves backward giving the impression that things are moving along, even when they are really not.

BUREAUCRACY,
OR "IT SAYS ON MY SCREEN"

See also *Dead Pens*.

As a general rule, you are not going to be whistling "Zip-A-Dee-Doo-Dah" in any situation that requires you to use a number to identify yourself. Americans spent almost 9 billion hours filling out government forms each year. Tax forms account for the bulk of that—according to one estimate, we spend a collective 6.1 billion hours on that alone. In spite of rosy predictions of the paperless office, the amount of paper we churn out continues to grow. Coopers and Lybrand estimate that there are over 4 trillion paper documents in the United States alone. But it is not drowning in paperwork that gets our goats, it is encountering impersonal, unyielding systems that make us feel like cogs in the wheel. The notion behind bureaucratic structures is highly democratic. It assumes that most people and situations follow similar patterns and that if rules are put in place to guide behavior, everything should run smoothly. The problem is, bureaucracy doesn't respond at all well to novel situations and it is not known for making compassionate, or even logical, exceptions to its rules.

We tend to think of a "bureaucrat" as a sort of job position. In truth, bureaucracy is a state of mind. A bureaucrat is a person with a personality and value system that says the letter of the law is meant to be followed regardless of logic or underlying circumstances—it says so right here on my screen. It is true that they are often found in government offices, but they can also be found at airports, deli counters, and coaching Little League. James H. Boren, author of *Fuzzify*, coined the collective noun "a mumble of bureaucrats" for them. As organizations become bigger and more impersonal, "rules are rules" systems and administrators become more and more prevalent. A bureaucrat is someone who does not feel he or she has the authority to make exceptions, and who likes not having that responsibility.

The people who are most frustrated by this mentality are those who can't get beyond the naïve belief that the underlying reality is supposed to matter. Go ahead. Keep believing that. It will cause you nothing but grief. Go write a rock song about "The Man" if you must, but your visa application will be denied if you send it to the address in the current printed instructions and not the one listed in the updated booklet that the Department of Homeland Security plans to print next year. (Seriously, don't get me started on this one!)

The best you can do is try to figure out how to use the letter of the law to your own advantage. As Gordon MacKenzie put it in his excellent little book *Orbiting the Giant Hairball* (the hairball being the bureaucratic office environment), "anytime a bureaucrat (i.e., a custodian of a system) stands between you and something you need or want, your challenge is to help that bureaucrat discover a means, harmonious with the system, to meet your need."

The biggest mistake you can make in trying to put an end to a bureaucratic standoff is to ask a bureaucrat to bend the rules. She wants to keep everything humming along properly. Rules keep us equal. You will not change such a person's core belief in the beauty and equality of the system. If you want to get what you want, you will have to be a little creative, and to think like a bureaucrat yourself. Rule books are thick, dense, and full of regulations that you can use in your favor.

Follow the example of Helen O'Neil. In the early 1980s, the artist found a home with a charming 125-year-old barn on a large lot in Rochester Hills, Michigan, an area that was quickly changing in character from rural to suburban. She thought the barn would make a wonderfully romantic pottery shed and workshop. After fixing it up, she put her works on display and started teaching pottery classes.

That's when the city government got involved. They ordered her to remove the "O'Neil Pottery" sign outside her property because a town ordinance prohibited commercial signs. Helen was undeterred. She had her name legally changed to "O'Neil-Pottery." There was no law against putting your own name on your mailbox or fence, was there?

CAR ALARMS ▶ CRINKLING CANDY WRAPPERS

CAR ALARMS

See also *Booming Car Stereos, Noise.*

It's 3 A.M. You are in the middle of that dream where you are flying over your childhood home when EEAAAEEEEAAAAEEEE . . . It's your neighbor's car alarm. Do you a) rush outside to foil the robbery in progress, b) immediately call the police, or c) put your pillow over your head and mutter "@#$% car alarms."

Chances are, you picked c. Separate studies in both New York City and Los Angeles found that 95 percent of the alarms are false. Smaller cities nationwide have had similar results. Everyone knows it, so no one pays much attention to the shrill sound—at least not as a warning. It is still very effective as a sleep deterrent.

"You have a car thief attacking your car. You're going to run out, and you're going to do . . . what?" vehicle security expert Reg Phillips asked a reporter for the *Atlantic.*

Annoyed woman

EEEAAAEEEAAAA

Bump by purse

DLX6

New York City councilpersons say there is no evidence that audible alarms deter auto theft. Experienced thieves can make off with your vehicle in a matter of seconds. One Los Angeles cop confessed that he put a car alarm only one step higher on his priority scale than "a car blocking a driveway."

Apparently in urban areas there are so many alarm-equipped vehicles, and they go off so often, no one recognizes the sound of his own car being invaded. To make it easier, alarm makers have made it possible for consumers to choose exactly what ear-splitting combination of tones they want. The wail is not only loud, it is designed to grate. It is high-pitched with repeating multi-tones. A typical siren has six tones so it can be customized . . . and infuriating.

A 2003 report estimated that New York's car alarms alone lead to about $400 to $500 million per year in "public-health costs, lost productivity, decreased property value, and diminished quality of life." Of course, this study was conducted by Transportation Alternatives, an organization that would like to see the city's cars replaced with bicycles.

To figure out just how annoying car alarms were they used the equation (V × APF) × (N × NDI) = 1 minute's worth of car alarm damage to the average New York City resident. V is the value of a New York minute, APF is the Aggravation Persistence Factor, N is noise, and NDI is the Noise Depreciation Index.

In spite of their questionable effectiveness, and the annoyance factor, audible car alarms remain the most common form of theft deterrent for vehicles. This is true in spite of the fact that there are low tech and quiet alternatives such as a steering wheel lock that are much more effective. There are now a number of high tech solutions as well, including car tracking systems that can lead police straight to a stolen vehicle and "immobilizers" that shut off the ignition unless you have a key with the right computer chip embedded in it. Of course, thieves are a crafty lot, and already they have found ways to hack alarm systems. It seems having to outwit criminals is the real aggravation.

CAR SEAT CONFUSION

See also *Some Assembly Required.*

You are an intelligent person with an advanced degree. Why does putting the child's car seat in make you want to tear your hair out? And how can you be sure you've done it right?

It's not just you. The editors of *Consumer Reports*, who test hundreds of child car seats in different vehicles each year, are equally challenged. "Even with our combined experience, we routinely find ourselves challenged by complicated car-seat instruction manuals and installations. If we're having such a hard time, we wonder, how would a parent who doesn't have much experience figure this all out?"

The answer, sad to say, is they don't.

In a recent study by the National Highway Traffic Safety Administration, new parents asked to install an infant seat did the job wrong between 95 and 100 percent of the time—95 and 100 percent! More experienced users fared a bit better, but even they put the seats in too loosely about half of the time. Most of them believed they had done it correctly.

You have probably heard the advice "when all else fails read the instructions." In this case, you will have to read two sets of instructions, those of the manufacturer of the car seat and your car's owner's manual. While most parents know enough to read the first, they don't realize that there may be pertinent information in the second manual as well.

The thing you're most likely to get wrong is leaving the seat too loose. When installed right, a child seat should move no more than one inch in any direction. There are two systems for attaching a car seat—the seatbelt system and what is known as a LATCH system. LATCH stands for "Lower Anchors and Tethers for Children." It was designed to make seat installation easier.

Either system is safe if done correctly. If you do use a LATCH system do not use a seatbelt installation too. This is not a case where more is better.

C

It is possible that your car's design is not helping you. A recent survey by the Insurance Institute for Highway Safety found that only about 20 percent of the popular vehicles they studied had hardware that made it easy to access the anchors that hold safety seats in place.

The second most common thing parents get wrong is putting the rear-facing infant car seat at the wrong angle. The seat should be set with a 30- to 45-degree angle in order to keep the baby's head back and prevent it from falling forward and obstructing the airway. If the seat does not have an adjustment knob you may need to put a rolled towel underneath to get it right.

As much as you'd like to look back and see your child's smiling face, do not switch to a forward facing car seat until your child is two years old or the maximum height and weight allowed by the car seat manufacturer. A child should stay in a forward facing car seat with a harness until he or she has reached the maximum weight—generally 40 to 80 pounds (18 to 36 kilograms). A booster seat should be used after that until the child reaches a height of 4 feet 9 inches (1.5 meters). After that it is safe to use just a safety belt.

Make sure your child is strapped in tight. If you can still pinch the fabric of the harness straps between your fingers, it is too lose. The straps should not have any slack.

If you are not sure you've done everything right—or even if you think you have—you can visit a car seat inspection event for help from the experts. The National Highway Traffic Safety Administration's homepage allows you to search for events by zip code.

CATS SHREDDING FURNITURE

See also Dogs Sniffing Your Privates, Fleas.

Some people have nice furniture—people without cats. You, on the other hand, have sofas with vertical rips that bleed stuffing. Sure, Fluffy is cute when she purrs, but when she scratches your furniture to bits you want to take about eight of her nine lives.

One of the reasons a cat scratches is to peel the old sheaths off its nails. Scratching also seems to be a form of exercise. Yet the most important reason Fluffy claws away may be to mark her territory.

The domestic cat has not strayed far from its wild origins. She may seem like a cuddly household pet, but in her mind, she is a big game hunter. In the wild, a cat has a large territory, depending on its gender. Males patrol about 150 acres and females about 15. They are looking for food and mates and trying to keep other cats away from their food and mates. Since you give your cat all the food she needs, and she has been spayed, she shouldn't need to obsessively mark and guard her personal space—but she still does.

T. S. Eliot got it right when he wrote a poem about the cat that was "always on the wrong side of the door." You let Fluffy out, two minutes later she is scratching at the window demanding to be let in. Two minutes after that, she is meowing at the door, ready to go back out.

"Cats are very territorial animals," says Betsy Lipscomb, president of Cats International. "They have to investigate every square inch of

Scratching helps to peel old layers of nails off claws

Fluffy

Your favorite couch

C their territory. They have to patrol it on a regular basis. Wherever their little paws have walked, that's now their territory. If the door is closed— they've been in that room before, they want to go in there and check it out on a regular basis. That's why they hate closed doors. It interferes with their job. They have a great duty."

Your cat requires the assistance of your opposable thumbs to get to the other side of that door, and she would rather have your begrudging help than wait around to check if there's a hideous beast lurking in part of her territory.

"Felines in general are dominant creatures," says California veterinarian Petra Drake. "Big cats such as lions and tigers are all basically at the top of the food chain with very little real threat of predator action against them. With this level of domination, big cats are able to exert tremendous control over their environment. Their movement in and around their territory is at will and constrained only by whim. Take this genetic endowment of environmental control and place it into a ten pound feline then stick in it a domestic setting. You get a wonderfully entitled creature who refuses to be constrained by a simple mechanical door handle." The scratching is part of this primitive impulse. It not only leaves a visible mark, it also leaves an odor for other cats to smell. The scent is secreted through glands in the cat's paws. This is why declawed cats keep trying to scratch. They are still able to spread their scent.

To change Fluffy's habits, you'll have to doctor your furniture for a little while. You can try putting double-faced masking tape on the corners of the furniture or covering the entire piece of furniture with a sheet. Where you put the scratching post is also important. Put it near the thing the cat most loves to destroy.

Gum sticking to shoe by van der Waals force

C

Gum on street

Your shoe

CHEWING GUM POLLUTION, OR GUMFITTI

You're on your first date with the cute red-haired guy you've had your eye on for weeks. He takes you to a sidewalk café. You're both smiling and chatting pleasantly until you cross your legs and the knee of your silk slacks gets stuck to the table by an oversize wad of dirty chewing gum that someone parked underneath. Not only are your slacks ruined, but the expletives coming out of your once sweet, feminine mouth have ruined any chance that you'll ever have children with freckles.

Americans didn't invent chewing gum. According to London's *Independent*, a university researcher named Elizabeth Aveling concluded from tooth marks in prehistoric tar that children have been chewing gum in northern Europe since about 7000 B.C. We have certainly taken to the habit, though. Modern chewing gum is made out of 40 to 50 compounds including pine tree resin, petroleum products, wax, and synthetic latexes. You're basically chewing a stickier version of the stuff they use to cover golf balls. It doesn't go

C

away, so when the sugar and flavorings have disappeared, the gooey lump has to go somewhere. It's surprising we're not all stuck in place from the gum on the soles of our shoes. If you take a good look at a city sidewalk you'll see black spots. That's ground-in, dirt-encrusted, already-been-chewed gum. It's expensive and time-consuming to remove. You can freeze it with Freon and scrape it up, smear it with citric acid-based chemicals and wait for it to dissolve, try to melt it away with hot water and chemicals, or "power-wash" it with pressures of 2,000 pounds per square inch. Sometimes this process damages the pavement without getting up the gum.

Gum is so sticky it almost defies the laws of physics. It is, in fact, about 10,000 times stickier than theoretical models say it should be. Chewing gum, like adhesive tape, owes its stickiness primarily to the van der Waals force, an electric force that acts between uncharged molecules. When experimenters measured the amount of energy needed to pull a metallic probe off a sticky surface, however, they discovered it took more force than would be needed to overcome van der Waals.

A pair of French researchers set out to find out why. Cyprien Gay, a physicist with the Centre National de la Recherche Scientifique in Paris, and Ludwik Leibler of Elf Atochem, a French Chemical company, devised a model that explains chewing gum's sticky behavior. When your shoe comes down on a piece of chewing gum, the boundaries of the rubber sole and the gum's surface come together. Air is trapped between them. As you pull your shoe away, the bubbles are stretched. They behave like tiny suction cups, which makes it harder to pull the gum away from the shoe and the shoe away from the gum.

The good news for public sanitation is that Americans, at least, are chewing less of the stuff than in days gone by. Gum sales in the United States have been declining since 2010. It all depends on where you live. Just as we are dropping the habit, chewers in China, Russia, and Mexico are taking up the sticky slack. Between 2009 and 2014, the global gum market grew 20 percent to about $24.7 billion. Let's hope our neighbors are better at finding trash cans.

Child 3-8 years old

Tattered children's book

Little Red Riding Hood

Father

C

CHILDREN'S STORIES OVER AND OVER AND OVER AND . . .

How many times does your child want you to read him *Clifford the Big Red Dog*? About fifty-seven more times than you want to read it. Your daughter, meanwhile, wants to see *Frozen* for the ninety-sixth time. Parents have been known to "lose" books, to suddenly "forget" how to read or speak English, or to "accidentally" back over the video with the car . . . five times in a row.

Listening to the same story over and over is part of the process that builds the neural pathways that form memory. As Peter Ornstein, professor of psychology at the University of North Carolina at Chapel Hill, explained in *Parenting* magazine, "The narrative form is the scaffolding and support for remembering." The first time a child hears a story or sees a movie, he starts to connect the elements of

C

the story to other experiences. Thus he creates new neural connections, but the connections are tenuous. To build stronger connections, he must reinforce it by repeating the experience.

"The child gets to connect these experiences with other kinds of experiences they've had by watching it over again," says Mary Mindess, a long-time professor of early childhood education at Lesley University in Cambridge, Massachusetts. "It makes those neural connections stronger and therefore able to branch out and make other kinds of connections. The story for them becomes more powerful each time they hear it."

There is also an emotional component. Favorite stories evoke strong emotions, joy, excitement, and catharsis. Children want to feel those emotions again, and they know they can do so by hearing the same story. "Young children like to have a sense of power," says Mindess. "The more they can hear the story, the more they can act the part of the story that gives them an additional sense of what they want to try to accomplish. Adults have more avenues for getting the repetition of the same emotional experience than the child has. The child doesn't have as many avenues to seek out, so he likes the repeat of things because he's pretty sure he knows what's going to happen."

The bad news is, there's not really anything you can do to rush through this stage of development. So buckle down and read *Green Eggs and Ham* one more time. The good news is, they do eventually grow out of it, and one day the book you couldn't stand to pick up will fill you with affectionate nostalgia.

CLICKWRAP:
BY READING THIS YOU AGREE
TO THE TERMS OF SERVICE

See also *Buffering, Computer Viruses, Pop-Up Ads, Trolls, Unfriended.*

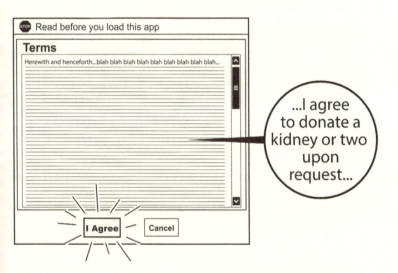

You are about to install that cool new app, sign up for an online subscription, or buy a book from an online retailer. Before you complete the transaction a screen appears in front of you with a scroll bar asking you to agree to the terms of service to continue. You read it right? Of course you don't. Nobody reads it.

We generally don't view these click-through documents as important information, but rather as an irritating obstacle to getting to the content or service we want. How do we know no one reads those agreements?

C

In 2016, a pair of researchers from two different universities did a little test. They created a fictional social networking site called NameDrop and had subjects sign up. Given the option, 74 percent of the study participants skipped over the privacy policy and opted for a "quick join." It took them, on average, 73 seconds to scan the privacy policy and 51 seconds to scan the terms of service. Based on average adult reading speed, if they had actually read and comprehended the material it should have taken a half hour to get through the privacy policy and 16 minutes for the terms of service. Lest you think they happened to have assembled a group of speed readers, there is further evidence that they skipped through the terms of service without reading it. The privacy policy said that anything posted on the network could be shared with the NSA "and other security agencies in the United States and abroad." It also said that your data could be shared with any third parties, and as a result noted that membership in the site could "impact eligibility in . . . employment, financial service, university, entrance, international travel, the criminal justice system, etc." And, in spite of the fact that the terms of service required the payment of "a first-born child" to access the service, fully 98 percent agreed. In a similar experiment in the UK in 2014, users were also willing to sign away their first-borns. A 2010 experiment conducted by a British retail site had users giving up their "immortal souls."

Yet the courts have held that so-called clickwrap is a legally binding agreement. You may not have read it, but you could have, and it is up to you to know what you are agreeing to. So clearly it behooves us to read the digital fine print. Here's the thing, we couldn't if we wanted to because we have lives. A team of researchers at Carnegie Melon University calculated that to read all of the various legal texts we encounter in a year would take twenty-five days. If you were to sit down and read them in eight-hour blocks, you'd need seventy-six work days to complete the task. Collectively that is 53.8 billion hours a year just reading terms of service and privacy policies. They estimate that if we actually did this, the value of the lost productivity would be $781 billion; that's more than the GDP of Florida.

Even if we had that kind of time, a lot of us could not make sense of the documents anyway. Researchers at Georgia Tech surveyed the terms of service agreements of the top thirty social media and fan sites and found that you need to possess the average reading level of a college sophomore to understand them. That means 60 percent of Americans do not have the education level required to make an informed decision before clicking.

The fact that we don't know what rights we've signed away leads to some paranoid meme sharing. There are periodic online waves of people posting a legal sounding status saying that the user does not grant Facebook the right to claim copyright over the birthday pictures and status updates you post. Various versions have circulated over the years. Don't share these things. They usually get the facts wrong, and, anyway, you can't unilaterally change the contractual terms you agreed to when you signed up to a service by posting something on your wall. The periodic outbreaks of these viral messages only goes to show that we'd rather click share than search out the actual privacy policy and read what's in it.

Is it fair that companies can create and legally enforce contracts that they know are not read? Probably not but the courts have spoken, and that is the way it is. There is a little bit of help out there. "Useable Privacy," a website launched jointly by Carnegie Mellon University and Fordham Law School, analyzes the privacy policies of various services and translates them into normal English so you don't have to. You can try it out at explore.usableprivacy.org.

COCKROACHES

See also *Ants, Fleas, Flies, Gnats, Mosquitoes.*

Y ou're trapped in your bed at night, afraid to step down and walk into the bathroom because there in the dark is your own personal horror movie. Hundreds of scuttling creatures, their feet making tiny click sounds.

If you dare turn on that light, you will see them zipping off into the corners and under the furniture. Even when you can't see them, you know they're there, somewhere, just waiting.

Cockroaches have been around for 350 million years and have evolved into about 3,500 separate species. They're hearty and highly adaptable. They have developed resistance to many household insecticides. They eat everything from grease spots to mold to each other, and they can get by without food for weeks. A female German cockroach, the species you're most likely to encounter in your kitchen,

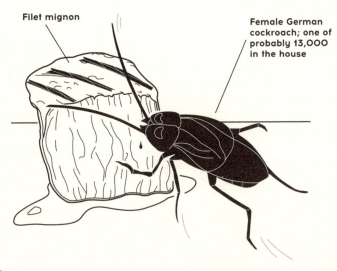

Filet mignon

Female German
cockroach; one of
probably 13,000
in the house

needs to mate only once. She is able to store enough sperm to fertilize all the eggs she will produce during her nine-month life span and produce about two hundred offspring. Some other cockroach species can reproduce without even mating through parthenogenesis—production of offspring from unfertilized eggs.

Philip G. Koehler, a professor of urban entomology at the University of Florida, conducted a survey of about 1,000 urban apartments for low-income tenants. Half had more than 13,000 cockroaches each. Heavily infested dwellings can contain 30,000 or more. Yet humans still hope against hope that we can wipe them out. Americans alone spend $1.5 billion a year spraying for cockroaches.

In case you needed a good reason to be grossed out by roaches, newly hatched German cockroaches survive the early days of life by eating the waste of the grown-ups. They never seem to lose a taste for excrement: older cockroaches eat their neighbors' waste. Researchers at the University of Florida at Gainesville have found that roaches find their way by following trails left by other roaches that defecate as they travel.

Assuming you do not want to share your home with roaches, one of the least toxic pest control chemicals is plain boric acid. Roaches haven't yet developed resistance to it. Put it into crevices and under sinks and appliances to keep the bugs at bay. If you prefer to avoid pesticides, try putting petroleum jelly on the inside of the mouth of a glass jar and putting bread inside as bait. The roaches fall in, but the jelly makes it too slippery for them to get out.

When roaches die, their legs stiffen and they fall sideways. They have a flat body with a high center of gravity, which is why they roll over when they keel over and you find them on their backs.

COFFEE SPILLS

See also *Cookie Mush*.

You make a fresh cup of coffee in the break room. You blow on it, take a quick sip and start to walk back to your office. How long will it take for you to slosh it all over your new blouse? About eight steps, say scientists. Coffee slosh is a simple case a fluid dynamics, and yes, University of California at Santa Barbara scientists have studied it using cameras and sensors on mugs. They calculated the natural frequency at which coffee sloshes back and forth when held in typical mugs of different sizes. They learned that coffee's frequency is the same as a person's natural gait. This causes the liquid to oscillate. Somewhere between the seventh and tenth step the coffee will slosh over the rim.

Some of your natural instincts make things worse. Coffee drinkers often try to walk quickly with their cups to get back to their desks before they spill, but the faster you move the closer your gait comes to the natural sloshing frequency of the coffee. You're better off walking slowly. Accelerate gradually. If you bolt away you'll create a big wave. You also want to avoid changing your pace. This results in wider oscillations or to put it in layman's terms—more sloshing.

Their scientific solution is to walk more slowly and to fill your mug less. Here is the formula: the gap between the top of the coffee and the rim should be at least one-eighth of the mug's diameter. If that doesn't work, there are always travel mugs with lids.

Of course, you don't need to be moving to make a mess with the joe. Is your desk covered in brown rings? You will be pleased to know that a number of years ago Robert D. Deegan, Sidney R. Nagel, and their coworkers at the James Franck Institute of the University of Chicago answered the age-old question, "Why does spilled coffee dry in an ugly ring?" The team published their findings in the journal *Nature* in an article called "Capillary flow as the cause of ring stains from dried liquid drops."

The researchers had puzzled over coffee rings for some time. They theorized that perhaps tiny electrical charges around the ring trapped the dissolved coffee particles, but when they did the math they found that it would take hours for the particles to form that pattern. Coffee dries much more quickly than that. They experimented by drying the drop upside down and putting it on clean silicon. They still got rings. The chemical composition of coffee could not be to blame because other liquids—tea, wine, milk—leave circles of their own.

Then one day a graduate student, Olgica Bakajin did an experiment of his own. Before a drop dried, he covered most of it. The part of the drop that had not been exposed to air did not form a ring. They theorized that the edge of the drop gets stuck because of irregularities in the table's surface, and surface tension keeps it in a drop shape. Liquid evaporates from the edge of the drop, where it thins and coffee from the center of the drop rolls outward to replace it. By the time it evaporates completely, almost all of the coffee has flowed to the edge.

To test their theory, the researchers suspended polystyrene spheres in a water droplet on a microscope slide. They videotaped the solution as it dispersed and, as predicted, it formed a ring. Next time someone comments on your coffee-stained counters, tell them you're just doing a science experiment.

COMMON COLD

See also *Coughing in the Theater.*

I t's not a big deal, it's just a cold. Not even worth calling in sick. You will just sit at your desk and hold your nose with a Kleenex while you fight the headaches, fever, and chills.

Different people have different reactions to colds. Most people, 95 percent, who are exposed to the rhino viruses that cause a cold do become infected, but only 75 percent get any symptoms.

People who are lucky enough not to feel sick fight off the infection just as well as you do with your runny nose and endless sneezing. Lucky them. Your dog and cat are immune to colds as well. The cold is only common to humans, chimpanzees, and higher primates. Feel better?

Cold viruses can live for a short time on a surface, say someone's hand. Shake hands with that person and you get the cold virus on your hand then you rub your nose and voila, the process begins. As little as a single particle of the virus is all that is needed to mount an infection. You breathe in and the virus, which contains strands of genetic coding coated in protein, is transported to the back of the nose by the nose itself. There it attaches itself to a receptor, which transports it into a cell in the respiratory track. Once it's in its cell, the virus can reproduce. More and more virus particles are created until finally the host cell bursts and the doses of virus infect new cells and the process starts anew. The whole thing takes about eight to twelve hours.

It takes about ten hours for the body to start mounting its defense. The inflammatory mediators histamine, kinins, interleukins, and prostaglandins cause your blood vessels to dilate so they can transport water and other materials needed to create extra mucus. Mucus is your nose's defense to just about any irritant. Unfortunately, the cold virus it is trying to flush out is hidden away safe within the walls of a nasal cell most of the time. However, the sneezing, coughing, and nose blowing do have one effect—they help to spread colds to

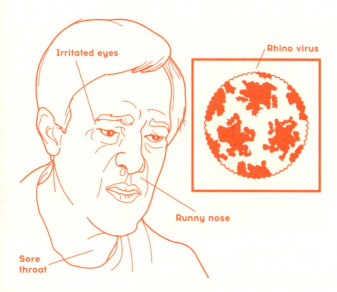

Irritated eyes

Rhino virus

Runny nose

Sore throat

other people.

There is some truth to the old wives' tale about chicken soup. If you're all stuffed up, the soup will loosen things up a bit; that is the conclusion of three clinicians who published the article "Effects of Drinking Hot Water, Cold Water and Chicken Soup on Nasal Mucus Velocity and Nasal Airflow Resistance" in the medical journal *Chest*. Hot chicken soup increased mucus velocity from 6.9 to 9.2 millimeters per minute, a result that is "statistically significant" compared to cold water and hot water. The faster the mucus velocity, i.e., how much mucus is expelled from the body, the faster the infected cells are expelled from the body (and spread to other people). The researchers concluded, "hot chicken soup, either through the aroma sensed at the posterior nares or through a mechanism related to taste, appears to possess an additional substance for increasing nasal mucus velocity." Go tell your mom she was right.

COMPUTER VIRUSES

See also *Buffering, Keyboard Crud, Trolls.*

Your computer is behaving strangely. Very strangely. You delete a file, and it seems to pop up again in another directory. Delete it again, it reappears somewhere else. There were a few documents in one file that you can't find anywhere now. What's going on? Suddenly a message pops up on your screen, "Super Hacker Strikes Again." You forgot to update your virus scanner's database, didn't you?

Being attacked by a computer virus is like being robbed or having your windows broken by a vandal. You feel violated, even if the virus did little damage. If it deletes files, rewords important documents, or causes your computer to crash, it can have far-reaching consequences.

According to Symantec, in 2015 nearly 317 million computer viruses were unleashed on the unsuspecting world. That is almost a million a day.

In the bad old days of early computing, computer viruses were often created by teenaged hackers who competed for bragging rights on how far their creations were able to spread in the wild. They were malicious pranks that relied on human nature to get people to download and execute email attachments and games with Trojan horses inside. If you're nostalgic for those simpler times, you can visit The Malware Museum's virus collection, which simulates (without the annoyance of actually going viral) some of the invasive coding from DOS days (archive.org/details/malwaremuseum&tab=collection).

The hackers of old wanted to take credit for their work, and their viruses were accordingly flashy. (One that affected this author replaced random words in Word documents with "wazoo.")

These days you're more likely to get a virus from a link on a social media site than from downloading an email attachment. The people who program viruses also have more sinister motives than their ancestors. A lot of them are trying to install keyloggers and other programs that steal your personal information, or they want to run in the background and use your computer as part of a network of spam marketing machines. An increasing problem is cyber ransom, where a tech-savvy blackmailer steals important data like photos or the only copy of your dissertation and then demands a ransom to unencrypt or return it.

These days, viruses often pass unnoticed. If your computer is suddenly running slowly or your hard drive is always spinning no matter how few resources you think you're using, there may be something going on in the background and it is time to run a virus/malware scanner.

I could end this entry with all of the standard advice about safe computing, keeping your antivirus definitions up to date, downloading the latest security updates on all your software, not downloading or clicking on content from strangers, or doing regular backups, but you have heard it all before. It is a constant battle between the forces creating malicious software and those creating the defenses against them. It is an annoyance that is not going to go away soon.

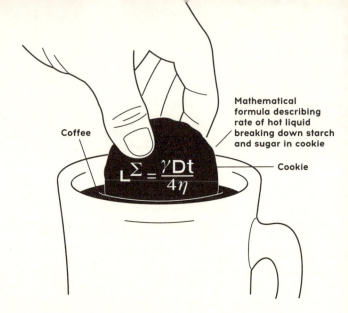

C

Coffee

Mathematical formula describing rate of hot liquid breaking down starch and sugar in cookie

Cookie

$$L\Sigma = \frac{\gamma Dt}{4\eta}$$

COOKIE MUSH AT THE BOTTOM OF YOUR MUG

See also *Coffee Spills, Crinkling Candy Wrappers.*

Cookies taste great when they're dunked in hot coffee, but leave them in the liquid too long and they crumble and end up as tasteless sludge at the bottom of your cup, depriving you of your sweet and ruining your morning pick me up. McVites, an English cookie manufacturer, studied the phenomenon and determined that about one-quarter of the cookies that are dunked into hot liquid end up as glop. In the process it splashes coffee in your face and all over your clean white shirt. Try to retrieve the cookie and you burn your fingers, spill the whole mixture on your lap, and spend the rest of the afternoon greeting clients as a mess of brown stains and bandages.

If you like to dunk, you'll be glad to know that researchers from the University of Bristol in England, after a two-month study employing high-tech equipment, discovered the mathematical formula that determines the ideal dunking technique and time to maximize the cookie-to-mush ratio.

Dr. Len Fisher and his team, being British, whimsically insist on calling cookies "biscuits" and focus primarily on the dunking of a crisp "digestive"-style confection into tea rather than the sensible American practice of dunking more porous (and tastier) chocolate chip cookies into coffee. Still, the scientific principles are the same.

Whatever you call them, cookies are starch held together by sugar. (Ok, so maybe "cookie" is actually a more whimsical term than "biscuit.") When a hot liquid enters its pores, the sugar melts and the structure becomes unstable. As this occurs, ten times more flavor is released than when you eat a dry cookie. That's why we do it. But, as Fisher told the BBC, "You have got a race between the dissolving of the sugar and your biscuit falling apart and a swelling of the starch grains so that they stick together, giving you a biscuit which is purely starch but rather softer than what you started with."

To determine the perfect dunking time, Fisher coated a digestive in twenty-four carat gold so he could scan it with an electron microscope and reveal its internal structure. Then he wet the cookies on one side and filmed the progress of the tea as it seeped in. Finally he used an Instron machine to measure how much the biscuit was affected by the moisture.

Using a mathematical formula—the average pore diameter in a cookie is equal to four times the viscosity of the hot liquid, multiplied by the height the liquid rises squared, divided by the surface tension of the beverage, multiplied by the length of time the cookie is dunked—Fisher determined that most English-style biscuits should remain in a hot drink for 3.5 seconds. He also revealed the perfect dunking technique. Using a wide-brimmed mug, the cookie should be dipped at a shallow angle and after the dunk, it should be rotated 180 degrees so the dry side supports the wet side. Of course the timing will be slightly different with the softer cookies we prefer on this side of the Atlantic. Fortunately for us, Fisher plans to publish a table which defines the ideal dunking times for various types of cookies.

COUGHING IN THE THEATER

See also *Crinkling Candy Wrappers*.

You're simply trying to hear the orchestra. Hack, hack, cough, cough, wheeze. Violins. Hacking. Cellos, throat clearing. Brass and phlegm. It bothers the performers, too. At a concert by the Carnegie Hall Jazz Band in Minneapolis, the musical director, Jon Faddis, stopped and chided audience members for their coughing.

In 1975, the Dallas Opera performed *Tristan und Isolde* and Jon Vickers, as Tristan, was lying flat on the stage while another singer was trying valiantly to be heard over a virtual cough concert. Vickers had enough and shouted: "Shut up with your damn coughing!" Opera singer Marilyn Horne once observed that the worst coughing occurs in cities with sunny climates, such as Dallas and Miami. In cities with long spells of damp, cold weather, the audiences are quiet.

Psychology may be as much to blame as itchy throats. During dramatic moments, when the audience is rapt, coughing subsides.

When the crowd becomes restless, the coughing resumes. Sometimes though, you just get that tickle in your throat and there's not much you can do. Many theaters have taken to providing free cough drops, but then there's the problem of unwrapping them. There's a trick to coughing in a theater without making noise. According to Florence B. Blager, chief of speech pathology and audiology service at the National Jewish Center for Immunology and Respiratory Medicine in Denver, you should not stifle the cough, but let the air explode outward. When you feel the cough begin, blow air through tightly pursed lips. This gets rid of the air a cough would expel without going through the vocal chords. We haven't tried this ourselves, but Blager insists it can be done with a little practice. If you don't develop this skill, Judith Martin, author of the syndicated "Miss Manners" column, says if you cough more than three times you should leave the theater.

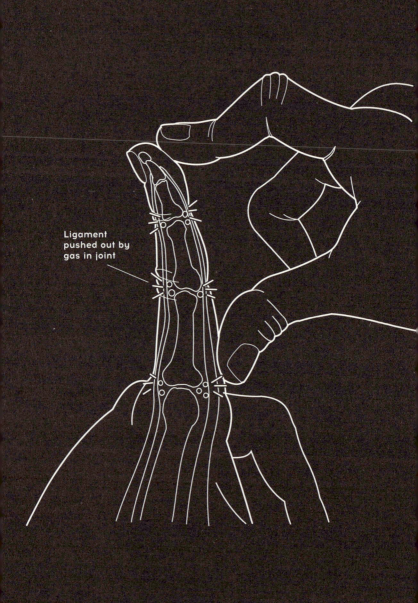

Ligament
pushed out by
gas in joint

CRACKING KNUCKLES

If you have a friend or coworker who habitually cracks his knuckles, you would probably like me to tell you that it causes cancer, AIDS, ozone depletion, and nuclear war. Anything that would scare the person enough to make him STOP. Sorry, I can't help you.

What happens inside the hands of a person who cracks his knuckles may be damaging to your nerves, but it's not particularly damaging to the knuckle cracker. Each joint is surrounded by fluid which fills the gap between the bones. Ligaments surround the whole thing and hold the joints together. When you put pressure on your finger, the pressure drops between the bones, and the ligament is pulled in by the small vacuum. At the same time, gas is forced out of the knuckle, forming a bubble. The bubble takes up the space between the bones, and the ligament snaps back into its original position with the familiar popping sound.

Contrary to popular belief, habitual knuckle cracking does not cause arthritis or deformed joints. As Dr. Dave Hnida told *CBS This Morning*, "Probably the biggest problem with cracking your knuckles is that it annoys everybody else that you're around." If you are looking for an honest reason to dissuade that knuckle-cracking neighbor, however, one study of people who had regularly cracked their knuckles over a period of thirty-five years showed they had slightly swollen joints and a weaker grip than nonknuckle crackers. If you're the one in the habit of cracking your knuckles, doctors recommend doing something else like squeezing a tennis ball, which will strengthen the muscles instead of weakening them.

C

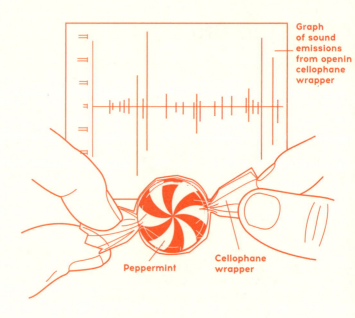

Graph of sound emissions from openin cellophane wrapper

Peppermint

Cellophane wrapper

CRINKLING CANDY WRAPPERS AT THE THEATER

See also *Coughing in the Theater.*

You're watching a movie—or trying to. The actors are speaking in hushed voices. "But if we set the fuse . . ." This is when the guy next to you decides it's time to open a wrapped piece of candy. Crinkle, crackle. "What about the alarm on the . . ." crinkle, crackle. "The most important thing is . . ." crinkle, crinkle, crackle, crink. This is when you stand up and shout, "Will you stop that?" A large usher personally escorts you out of the theater.

Whether you're trying to enjoy the show next to a snacking

audience member or you're the snacking culprit trying in vain to unwrap a hard candy without attracting attention, those crinkling wrappers are irritating. Fortunately, a pair of scientists has devoted considerable mental energy to answering the question: "Is there a way to open a plastic wrapper in a theater so that it makes less noise?" Unfortunately, the answer to that question is "no."

It was a fortuitous accident that turned Eric Kramer of Simon's Rock College in Great Barrington, Massachusetts, and Alexander Lobkovsky of the National Institute of Standards and Technology in Gaithersburg, Maryland, into pioneers in the field of annoying candy wrapper research. They were graduate students at the University of Chicago when they began studying crumpled plastic membranes, hoping their investigations would yield some positive uses in automobile safety, the efficient design of packaging materials, and the properties of two-dimensional polymers.

They began by crumpling a sheet of polyester film thirty to forty times to make permanent creases. They then made high-resolution digital recordings of the sounds that were produced as they uncreased it. They discovered that the physics of candy wrappers is highly complex. When a flat plastic wrapper is twisted around a piece of candy, it is permanently changed. The creases—the scientists call them disorder in the curvature of the material—are responsible for the noises you hear.

When you think you're just unwrapping a piece of candy, you're actually moving the plastic from one stable configuration to another stable configuration. Every time you do this there is a corresponding click. The sound is not continuous. It is made up of pops that last only a thousandth of a second. The loudness of the random pops has nothing to do with the speed at which you twist the wrapper or even the thickness of the material. In other words, no matter how you do it, it's going to make the same amount of noise.

The best expert advice Kramer and Lobkovsky can give is to open the candy as fast as you can and get it over with.

D

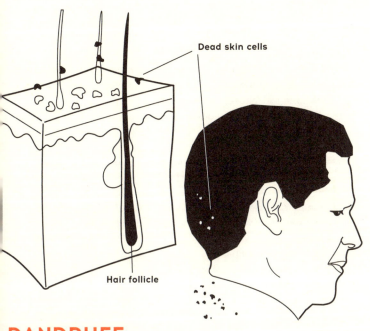

Dead skin cells

Hair follicle

DANDRUFF

See also *Dust Coating Your Computer Monitor.*

T hat little itch could be telling them you have dandruff. Or it could be the fact that your shoulders look like ski slopes, or that you have a bald spot from unremitting clawing at your scalp . . .

Dandruff is very common—about 50 to 60 million Americans have it. Dermatologists have come to discover that it may be yet another problem caused by an imbalance in the ecosystem of tiny creatures that live on your body. Your scalp is home to a yeastlike organism called Pityrosporum ovale (P. ovale for short). Climate, hormones, and other factors can provide a more fertile landscape for P. ovale. Some people's skin overreacts to the presence of these guys. The immune system kicks in and responds by overproducing skin cells which are renewed up to ten times faster than normal.

D Some scientists, however, think the greater presence of P. ovale is the effect, rather than the cause of the increased skin production.

Whatever the cause, the more skin cells are made, the more shed. You are always shedding skin, about 400,000 particles a minute, but the skin cells that fall from other parts of your body are so small we only notice them when they accumulate on our computer screens as dust. Your scalp produces more oil than other parts of your body. This binds the skin particles together producing flakes.

The ICR Survey Research Group (now SSRS) of Pennsylvania questioned 700 people with dandruff. About 21 percent of those surveyed said they'd rather have a headache than dandruff.

Another 17 percent would take heartburn over dandruff. Ten percent said they'd be happier during an allergy attack, and 9 percent said they'd gladly exchange it for athlete's foot.

If your dandruff is less pronounced, you are still probably embarrassed about it, thanks to television commercials that tell you you're supposed to be. Half of the survey respondents were self-conscious about it. Men, it turned out, worried more than women—58 percent of the men and 48 percent of the women were as concerned about what other people think as they were about the condition itself.

If you are worried about your wintry shoulders, dandruff shampoos do work. In fact, a recent study showed that over-the-counter dandruff shampoos were as effective as prescription dandruff shampoos. (This is good because it means the over-the-counter stuff is as effective as anything else, but bad because if Head and Shoulders doesn't cure your case of dandruff there's not really anything much better out there.) The main ingredients in dandruff shampoos are zinc pyrithione, selenium sulfide, salicylic acid, and coal tars. The active ingredients either retard cell growth (cytostatic) or they loosen and remove cell overgrowth (keratolytic). Some new dandruff shampoos (like Nizirol A-D) employ an antifungal ingredient, ketoconazole, which kills P. ovale.

DEAD PENS

You are listening to your favorite radio station when the announcer says, "In just a moment we will give out the telephone number and one lucky caller will win one million dollars." You grab a pen and the announcer starts rattling off digits. You run the pen across the paper but nothing comes out. You draw circles and squiggles. You tear a hole in the page but still no ink. By now the announcer is saying, "Congratulations! You're our tenth caller!" You could have been a millionaire were it not for a ballpoint pen malfunction. Bleeping pens!

Before you curse that implement any further, take a moment to appreciate just what a revolutionary invention the pen was. You could have been looking for a knife to sharpen the end of your quill when that contest was announced. Laszlo Biro's 1938 creation combined a ball bearing and fast-drying ink, eliminating the need for messy ink wells or cartridges. In fact, there is an entire book on this groundbreaking invention, *Ballpoint* by György Moldova.

Now that you've pondered the miracle that is a working ballpoint, here are a few suggestions to fix its nonworking counterpart. First, open the cap on the back of the pen and slide the cartridge out to make sure there is actually ink in it. If there is no ink, none of the other tips will do you any good.

One of the most common problems is a ball that has become stuck. If drawing circles fails to get the ball moving, try tapping the tip on a hard surface. This brings the ink down to the point and helps loosen the ball. If that doesn't work, heat the tip of the pen with a lighter. Be sure to keep the tip over the flame for only a couple of seconds, otherwise you might melt the pen. Another method is to dampen a bit of paper towel with rubbing alcohol and wipe the tip of the pen to remove any dried ink.

Sometimes the problem is not a stuck ball but air pockets between the tip and the inkwell. You can solve this problem with centrifugal force using a fun helicopter method. Place the pen in the center of a rubber band. Tape the band to the side of the pen, so that the pen is inside the circle. Using your index fingers, pull on both ends of the rubber band then flip the pen so the rubber band winds up. When it is well wound, release the pen and let it spin to redistribute the ink.

This is also something you can do to keep from getting bored during business calls. If your boss walks by, just say you're trying to get the ink flowing.

Incidentally, have you ever noticed that a lot of plastic pen lids have a hole at the top? This design feature was implemented to increase air flow—yours. You see, an awful lot of people mindlessly chew or suck on the ends of their pens. No one has studied exactly how many of us do this, but they do know that about one hundred people a year die after they've accidentally swallowed the things. Pen makers responded by putting holes in the top to allow air to pass even if a lid becomes lodged in the throat. Pen makers are life savers. Now, don't you feel bad about complaining?

DOGS SNIFFING YOUR PRIVATES

See also *Cats Shredding Furniture*.

You have planned your dinner party for months. You've invited a potential new client and her husband. You spent hours cooking, setting the table with the best flatware, the soft music is playing, and you open the door only to have Fido make a beeline for your guest's privates and nestle his nose right between her legs.

Why does your dog embarrass you this way? Instinct. It is perfectly normal dog behavior. (As, incidentally, is humping other dogs, inanimate objects, and your leg. The ASPCA has a web page devoted to "Mounting and Masturbation" if you want to know more about that.) Fido is not trying to be rude. He probably thinks you're the impolite one when you push him away as he is trying to get to know your guest. A dog's strongest sense is smell. When one dog encounters another, he sniffs around to get information the way you or I would scan someone's face. We look for fine lines and wrinkles to determine a person's age, hairstyles, and facial characteristics to determine gender, and a whole host of visual cues to tell us about someone's mood. Dogs can glean all of that with a quick whiff.

D   We can't because we lack the receptor cells known as the vomeronasal organ or Jacobson's organ that your dog has just above the roof of his mouth. It has ducts that open to the mouth and nose and convey information to the brain thanks to a rich network of blood vessels and nerves. The dog's brain has a much more developed olfactory bulb to interpret this wealth of information.

The sweet spot for smelling is the apocrine gland, a sweat gland that produces pheromones. These are highly concentrated in mammals' genital and anal regions. And if this was not humiliating enough, there are certain scents that are almost guaranteed to draw extra canine attention. In case you think I am making an unwarranted assumption here, you should know that scientists have tested this. In a study "Behavioural variability of olfactory exploration of the pet dog in relation to human adults," Filiatre et al. tested whether dogs were really more interested in the scent of strangers or whether their owners had trained them to keep away from their private parts. They dressed up dolls with clothing worn by a familiar person and to an unfamiliar person. The dogs consistently gave more attention to the unfamiliar scent than the familiar. The researchers conclude that ignoring owner's genitals was not a learned behavior.

Dogs are especially drawn to the privates of people who have recently had sex, who are menstruating, or who have recently given birth. They are also able to detect ovulation. A team of Australian researchers trained dogs to identify cows that had recently ovulated in order to help farmers successfully breed them.

Canine genital sniffing makes us blush a little, but most of us understand that this is instinctive behavior. Some people, however, are absolutely mortified when it happens. Once a Connecticut woman sued the owner of a Golden Retriever named Kodak for sexual harassment after Kodak sniffed under her skirt. Her lawyers argued that the owner was complicit because he did nothing to stop it. The case was dismissed. As the judge later told a reporter, "Impoliteness on the part of a dog does not constitute sexual harassment on the part of the owner."

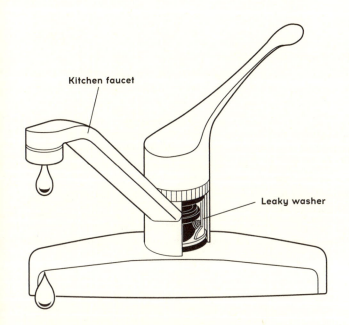

Kitchen faucet

Leaky washer

DRIPPING FAUCET

Drip. Drip. Drip. Drip. It's water torture. Pure water torture.

That is, if you're a woman. You probably have conversations that go like this: "Honey, I thought you said you were going to fix that faucet?" "Yeah. I'm going to get around to it. What's the big deal?" "Isn't that dripping driving you crazy?" "I said I'd get to it. Jeez."

"A dripping faucet falls into a class of aggravating things that is more aggravating to women than to men," says Francis T. McAndrew, professor of psychology at Knox College in Galesburg, Illinois. "They notice them quicker and are bothered by them more. A man is more likely to say 'what noise?'"

The sound of water itself is not irritating. In fact, the sound of a waterfall or a babbling brook is relaxing; but you'll never find a New

D Age "nature sounds" CD with the title "faucet drip." The dripping faucet, unlike the waterfall, is a sign that something is wrong. It's the constant reminder that something in the home is broken.

"It nags at you because it's not supposed to be there," McAndrew says. "It's a signal that there's something amiss and you can't quite relax and forget about it because there's something that needs to be fixed or water's being wasted or whatever is bothering you."

As to why women are more bothered than men, McAndrew speculates that it has to do with our "hunter-gatherer" roots. "Women and men are just primed to tune into different things," he says. "There is quite a bit of evidence that women are much better at remembering the location of objects. The hypothesis is that women were the gatherers so they were better at remembering the locations of things," and presumably to little things that are amiss in the home environment, like that infernal dripping faucet.

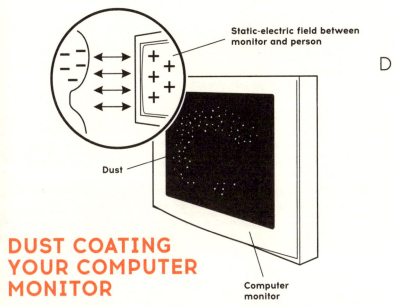

Static-electric field between monitor and person

Dust

Computer monitor

DUST COATING YOUR COMPUTER MONITOR

See also *Dandruff.*

Why is it that no matter how many times you get up and wipe off the screen, you're always running your spreadsheet program through a haze of dust?

Technically, there isn't really such a thing as a "dust molecule." Dust can be just about anything as long as its particles are small enough to be carried through the air—less than one-tenth the width of a human hair. Dust is everywhere. It lands on every surface on just about every part of the planet.

Dr. Joseph Prospero, a professor of atmospheric chemistry at the University of Miami has been studying dust for more than thirty years. His discoveries may give you a new appreciation for the snowy coating on your monitor.

Outdoor dust is made up largely of particles of rock that take to the air as wind and water erode mountains. Prospero found that the red dust that fills the air in many East Coast states comes all the way from

D   Africa. Bermuda's islands would not have top soil were it not for blowing African dust. Some terrestrial dust even comes from outer space; it is deposited into our atmosphere by comets and brought home by gravity.

Indoor dust is a different matter: some is tracked in from the outside, but most is created in the house. About forty pounds of dust accumulates in the average household each year. As you may have heard, most of it is made up of your own skin. Human beings shed about 400,000 particles a minute according to chemist and dust expert Armin Clobes.

Clobes is a senior research associate for SC Johnson Wax. He uses electron microscopes and lasers to analyze the content of household dust. Our dust is a microscopic version of everything we keep in the home—carpet fibers, food particles, dead bugs, hair, pet dander, and clothing lint.

Given the right conditions, dust can even create dust. If there is enough moisture in the air, mold and bacteria grow in piles of dust and create their own dust clouds. All of this is enough to make the housekeeper throw in the towel, but it is important to try to keep household dust at bay. It provides food for dust mites, a distant relative of the spider. Their waste products can trigger allergic reactions.

Electronics like your computer, television, and stereo carry an electric current that generates a field of static energy. Because most dust particles carry an electrical charge, they cling to other charged surfaces. (Sometimes they cling to each other and form dust bunnies.) A dust particle that might just fall off a table sticks to an electronic device because of this attraction.

According to *Electronic Design* magazine, the trajectories of the charged dust particles are influenced by the electric fields between a television or computer monitor and the viewer. Thus, the same coating you see on the screen can accumulate on your face. When you walk away, however, the electrical field is broken and some of the dust will fall off. And you do wash your face more often than you clean your monitor, don't you?

E

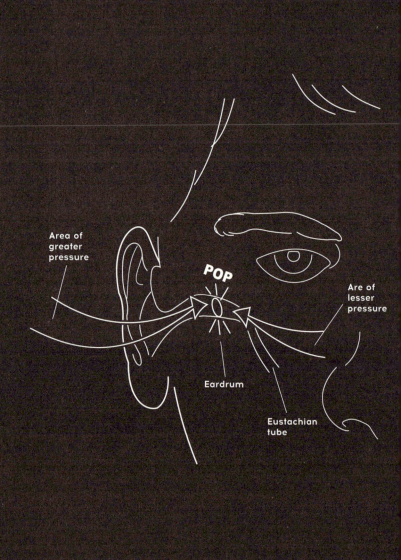

EARS POPPING IN AIRPLANE

See also *Airplane Legroom, What Does It Really Cost?*

The airplane heads up into the clouds and suddenly you have the sensation of cotton being shoved into your ears—from your skull out. The pilot is giving a safety message, but to you it sounds like the adults in a "Peanuts" cartoon. If you have a cold, you're treated to pain as well.

Fast changes in altitude make your ears feel puffed up and blocked. Scientists have a name for this; they call it barotitis or aerotisis. At sea level, the air pressure in your middle ear is equal to the air pressure that surrounds your head. The higher you go, however, the lower the air pressure becomes. So air flows out of the ear through the Eustachian tube and into the nose and throat.

When the plane stops ascending and levels off, your body has a chance to put things back into balance by letting out enough air so your ear pressure matches cabin pressure. Your ears feel fine again until it's time to land. The whole process is reversed as the plane goes down and the air pressure in the cabin increases. Now there is a greater pressure outside than inside your middle ear. The air tries to force its way back into the ear through the Eustachian tube. If it has trouble, say you have a head cold that irritates the tiny tube and keeps it shut, you may feel pain.

The best way to keep barotitis at bay on the way up is to equalize ear pressure by swallowing. It opens the Eustachian tube and makes it easier for the extra air to escape. This is why people suggest chewing gum. Sipping water or chewing on a snack can serve the same purpose. If that doesn't work, *Prevention* magazine suggests swallowing while holding your nose. This creates a small vacuum that draws pressure from the middle ear.

When you head back down, *Prevention* suggests gently blowing air into your nostrils while holding your nose. This technique has a name— the Valsalva maneuver. It forces air into the middle ear.

F

FARTS

You digest, you create gas. Simple as that. Everyone does it—an average of ten times a day. Certain foods are infamous for their gas-producing ability. Beans, broccoli, cabbage, and apples contain complex sugars that can't be broken down by digestive juices. Bacteria in the intestines ferment them and the result is gas. You'll be pleased to know that scientists have devoted a great deal of mental energy to the study of farts. In 1967, for example, The New York Academy of Sciences held an entire two-day conference on the subject of gastrointestinal gas. A pair of Australians, gastroenterologist Terry Bolin and nutritionist Rosemary Stanton, wrote a book, *Wind Breaks*, on the subject. It is now in its third printing.

The top researcher today is probably Dr. Michael Levitt, chief of research at the Minneapolis Veterans Administration Hospital, who has been studying our emissions since 1965. He has learned that some people pass gas more often and others pass larger volumes less often, but the total volume remains roughly the same, up to

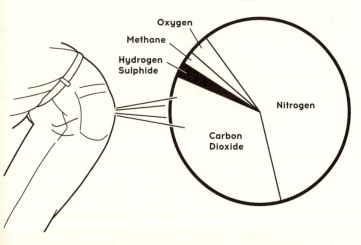

Oxygen
Methane
Hydrogen Sulphide
Nitrogen
Carbon Dioxide

2,000 milliliters, or about 120 cubic inches of gas a day. Frequency depends on the sensitivity of the walls of the rectum. The more sensitive it is to distension the more frequently it will release the emissions. With age, the bowel becomes less elastic and more sensitive to being distended, thus older people fart more frequently, but continue to have the same overall output of gas.

Most of it is odorless. Only 1 part in 10,000 is stinky. It is primarily made up of nitrogen, oxygen, carbon dioxide, hydrogen, and methane. The first two ingredients are swallowed while eating. When you belch it is mostly made up of these swallowed gases so it doesn't smell as bad as the stuff that comes out the other end.

The rest of the ingredients in intestinal gas are produced in house. Half of it comes from what we eat. The rest comes from our bile and the mucus and linings of the intestines. Levitt and his team dressed volunteers in gas-tight Mylar pants and collected their gaseous output then filtered it until the subjects reported it no longer smelled bad. They learned that the distinctive smell comes from hydrogen sulfide, methanethiol, and dimethyl sulfide. Sulfur is the key ingredient in all of them.

If you've ever described a particularly nasty fart as "lethal," you were not that far off. The gases are similar chemically to the odorant added to natural gas so we can detect leaks. The brain apparently has the same thing in mind when it reacts to the fragrance. The sulfur-based gases are highly toxic, Levitt says, so we have evolved to detect them at very low levels. The brain perceives of the scent as offensive so we try to get away from it. Don't have to tell me twice.

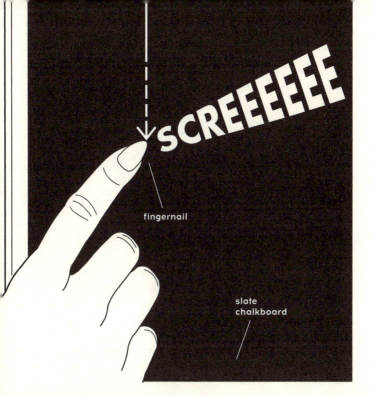

fingernail

slate
chalkboard

FINGERNAILS ON A BLACKBOARD

See also *Off-Key Singing*.

The world is full of annoying sounds—crying babies, car horns, a bagpipe, and didgeridoo concerts—but the king of them all has to be the sound of fingernails on a blackboard. It is so universally despised it has become a metaphor for awful noise and anything that frays the nerves. What makes the high-pitched scrape so difficult to hear? Believe it or not, scientists have devoted a fair amount of attention, energy, and resources to this perplexing question, but they have yet to come to a consensus.

F

Researchers Lynn Halpern, Randy Blake, and Jim Hillenbrand of Northwestern University investigated the "psychoacoustics of a chilling sound" by having twenty-four adult volunteers listen to noises and report their reactions. As expected, the subjects almost all cringed at the blackboard sound. The research team suspected that it was the high-pitched portion of the sound that made listeners shiver. They filtered it out and played the remaining sound to their subjects. To the researchers' surprise, they discovered that the volunteers still found the sound unpleasant. Interestingly, when they removed the lower pitched portion of the sound, the volunteers didn't mind it.

William Yost, president of the Parmly Hearing Institute at Loyola University, speculates that the reason people found the second recording bearable was that they no longer recognized it as fingernails on a blackboard and that it is the image of actually running one's fingernails down the slate surface of a blackboard that creates the discomfort, not the sound itself. The Northwestern team has its own theory. They compared the wave forms of fingernails on a blackboard with those of the warning cries of macaque monkeys. They found there was a strong resemblance. Randy Blake wrote in *Psychology Today*, "We speculate that our spine-tingling aversion to sounds like fingernails scraped over a surface may be a vestigial reflex."

FLAT BEER

See also *Coffee Spills, Cookie Mush.*

I t was so refreshing, that first sip of frothy, cold beer on a summer afternoon. Now it's warm and bitter with nothing but a little white circle on top where the foam used to be.

Beer is fizzy because of carbon dioxide, which is generated either by the action of yeasts and sugars in the drink or added at the brewery. In a can, bottle, or keg, the CO_2 is kept inside because of the pressure of the container. When the container is opened, the pressure drops and gas escapes.

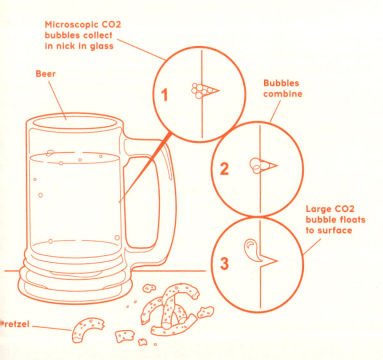

Microscopic CO2 bubbles collect in nick in glass

Beer

1

Bubbles combine

2

Large CO2 bubble floats to surface

3

Pretzel

F

If you pour your beer into a glass, or if it is contained in a sufficiently clear bottle, you will see tiny bubbles rising to the top in streams along the inside of the glass surface. The bubbles seem to emanate from invisible points. Even though the glass appears to be smooth, the surface has tiny nicks and crevices in it. These hold air pockets, which attract molecules of carbon dioxide. Carbon dioxide is attracted to both the liquid and the air pocket, so it is suspended there for a time. Finally, the air pocket wins out and CO_2 molecules cling together along the surface of the crevice. Once the bubble becomes too buoyant to be held down, it breaks away and rises to the surface and a new bubble starts to form.

At the top of the liquid, the bubbles form foam—the head on a mug of beer. Eventually, the bubbles burst and the head collapses. The bubbles burst faster if they come into contact with fat. Lipstick and the oil on your skin can thus deflate the froth.

Cold liquids can hold more carbonation than warm liquids, so as your beer warms up, its ability to hold CO_2 decreases. More of the gas escapes to the surface and dissipates. Eventually there are no bubbles left.

A team of British researchers from the Institute of Food Research (IFR) in Norwich and Brewing Research International in Surrey have taken on the vital task of beer-head preservation. The scientists are studying some of the proteins in barley (an ingredient in beer) that protect the plant from attack by pathogens. "It was something of a surprise to discover that they might also prove very useful in counteracting the effects of crisp-eating on beer foam," an IFR press release said.

They discovered that some of these proteins contain a pocket which can "mop up" fat molecules and keep them from bursting the foam bubbles in beer. Once they figure out exactly how the process works, they hope to be able to make recommendations on brewing methods to keep you in suds.

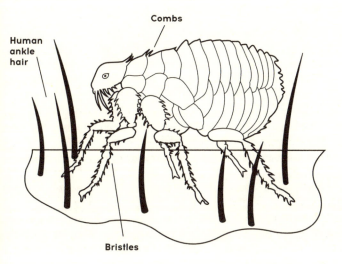

Human ankle hair

Combs

Bristles

FLEAS

See also *Ants, Cockroaches, Flies, Gnats, Mosquitoes.*

Fido's foes are all over your house. The dog is scratching its fur off. You can't walk through the carpet without little insects jumping at your heels. Need any more reason to hate fleas?

How about this—their mass murdering ancestors killed off a quarter of Europe's population by spreading the bubonic plague during the Middle Ages. There are about 1,600 species of fleas in the world. The medical entomologist John W. Maunder once said he has evidence of a "vast flea epidemic" throughout Western Europe and much of the United States. In all, the world's fleas probably weigh more than the world's humans. If your cat has fleas, there may be only a dozen or two on the animal. Another 10,000 may be hiding out in the carpet waiting for a warm-blooded host to walk by.

All are tiny, wingless insects with a taste for blood. Their bodies are fortified with a row of spines above their mouthparts (on their back). These are called the combs or ctenidia. Entomologists used to believe these helped the fleas move through fur or feathers. Now they believe the setae, bristles on the legs, help them move while the combs make it difficult for you to pluck them out of your pet's fur. If you've ever tried to do this, you've seen firsthand how effective they are. Fleas' hard, pointy heads are perfect for burrowing, and their mouthparts allow them to pierce skin and suck blood.

They measure between .04 to .4 inches in length. Don't let their diminutive size fool you—they're strong. If you had the jumping ability of the flea, you could leap to the top of a twenty-five-story building in a single bound—30,000 times in row. (Men: if you were "hung like a flea," you'd have a pair of penises.) Some fleas are picky eaters, preferring the blood of only one species, but others will snack on another creature if their preferred host is unavailable—cat fleas fall into this category. Fluffy's fleas will bite you in a pinch. The most popular mammals, though, are rodents. Fleas love rats.

They're not nearly as fond of horses, monkeys, apes, and humans. Flea's eggs are the size of a pinhead. If your pet is infested, you can probably see them in the fur. They look like specks of dirt. When they hatch, mom and dad feed the larvae with their blood-rich feces (yum!). If their parent's droppings aren't available, they eat one another. The larva make cocoons and, depending on the species, they stay there for a few days or months. Then they emerge as fully grown adults ready to suck some blood.

No fleas in your home? You can go look at them in a museum. The largest flea collection in the world is housed in the British Museum in London. There are also collections at the Canadian National Museum in Ottawa and at the Smithsonian in Washington D.C.

FLIES

See also *Ants, Cockroaches, Fleas, Gnats, Mosquitoes.*

I t buzzes around your ear, taunting you. It knows you won't get it with that swatter. You swat, swat, swat and it just laughs at you with that little fly bzzzzz. The reason the fly always seems to get away is that its compound eyes give the insect the ability to respond to light ten times faster than we can. It sees that swatter coming and flies away with wings that beat about 180 times a second (that's also what causes the buzzing sound). Are you ready to give up and move to Alaska? Forget it—the common housefly, *Musca domestica*, flies EVERYWHERE there are human beings. They're in Alaska and in deserts. One trash can may serve as a breeding ground for more than 30,000 maggots a week. (Nope, they're not even cute as babies.) Depending on which expert you ask, there are between 120,000 and more than a million different kinds of flies in the world. They can walk upside down on ceilings with glands on their feet that produce a sticky substance.

F

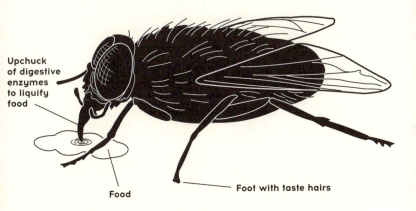

Upchuck of digestive enzymes to liquify food

Food

Foot with taste hairs

Flies can also taste with those feet. They have 1,500 taste hairs, which can savor the flavor of a sugar cube or a cow patty, two fly favorites. To be fair, flies don't actually eat dung. That would be gross. They drink the moisture from it. This is because flies urinate every few minutes and they need to replenish the liquid regularly.

Adult flies can't chew. They sponge up food. That means they have to convert whatever they eat into liquid. They do this by throwing up. Put another way, they expel digestive enzymes onto food to start breaking it down before they eat it. Then, with the help of a pumping organ in the head, they suck up the liquid using a spongelike mouth part. If you're not sufficiently irritated by flies now, here's yet another reason to dislike them: flies have been known to carry such diseases as typhoid fever, cholera, dysentery, trachoma, and anthrax, which they spread with their unique feeding habits.

There is one piece of good news about flies. Baby flies—that is maggots—have medical uses. As creepy as the idea may seem, many doctors are using the larvae to eat away dead infected tissue from wounds. They eat the infected tissue while sparing healthy tissue. There is also evidence that maggots exude antibacterial chemicals such as allantoin. Physicians put a quantity of maggots—from a dozen to a hundred or so—into an infected wound and keep them in place with a dressing designed to protect intact skin from the potent enzymes produced by the maggots. An average dose of larvae can digest around 14 grams of dead tissue a day. Yum.

FOOT'S ASLEEP
AND FOOT CRAMP

You've been sitting for a while when . . . pins and needles . . . pins and needles in your foot. If your foot is asleep, it must be having nightmares. Feet do not "fall asleep" because the circulation has been cut off. If your circulation is interrupted, the result is a leg cramp. A foot falling asleep is irritating. A leg cramp is painful. What happens during a cramp is that a calf or foot muscle goes into spasm and shuts down the blood flow, depriving muscles of oxygen.

A sleeping foot has nothing to do with your veins. A foot usually falls asleep when you've been sitting cross-legged. The peroneal nerve, which runs through the knee and sends messages from the foot to the brain, becomes compressed. As a result, your brain gets all kinds of screwy messages about the "foot," which is actually perfectly fine. People often stand and stomp their feet trying to "restore circulation." It does work, but not for the reasons they think. By standing you stretch the nerve back to its normal shape and the odd signals stop.

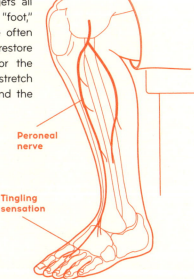

Peroneal nerve

Tingling sensation

FREE TIME? WHAT FREE TIME?

I can't talk now, I have to pick up the kids and take them to band practice and cook dinner and work on my report for tomorrow's annual meeting and mend my jacket and learn French and, wait, a text just came in from my boss, he wants me to send off that report to a client in Tokyo . . .

As late as the 1980s, forecasters were predicting that by 2000 our biggest problem would be what to do with the almost unlimited leisure time technology would grant us. By 1999 the tune had changed. That year, an issue of *American Demographics* magazine predicted that: "The cry of the needy in the new millennium may well be 'Brother, can you spare some time?'"

In the new century something even more damaging to free time occurred. Our home computers became laptops and then phones, pads, and watches. You can always be reached, and the boundaries between home and work, vacation and responsibility began to blur.

Some experts believe we're not actually any more pressed for time than previous generations, we just believe we are. Time-use experts John P. Robinson and Geoffrey Godbey's book *Time for Life* asserts that Americans have almost five hours more free time per week than in the 1960s. In fact, we average about forty hours of free time per week (away from work, meals, housekeeping chores, child care, and sleep). Yet most estimate they have about sixteen hours a week of free time.

As people feel more stressed, they tend to misreport the length of time at work to a greater degree. They use "lack of time" as a shorthand for feeling stressed. Godbey believes we feel more rushed because twenty-five of our forty hours of leisure time fall on weekdays and come in chunks of an hour or two, he claims. "In many cases, that time does not provide for psychological release. If leisure means tranquility, these hour-long chunks may not have much effect."

Constant device checking does not help. At work, one study found that 70 percent of emails were opened within six seconds, and it took a minute per interruption for the recipient fully to regain concentration. That might be okay if we left work at work, but we don't. A survey conducted by Adobe Software found that 87 percent of employees check emails outside of work. Another survey found that 61 percent of us do work while on vacation. Yet another survey, this one by a mobile-software firm, found that 68 percent of people checked work email before 8 A.M., 57 percent checked on family outings, 38 percent at the dinner table, and half of us check email even in bed. On average we spend about 6.3 hours reading and responding to emails each day. If you are checking work emails during commercials, at the gas station, or when you're waiting for the movie to start, your leisure becomes increasingly fragmented and unsatisfying. Increasingly, when researchers ask, people tell them that they would be willing to earn less money in exchange for more free time.

Another reason for our obsession with time is that as our roles in society become less rigid, more and more of our position in life is

F

determined by portable skills and credentials. Therefore, to increase our value in our chosen careers and society, we need to chalk up many measurable accomplishments. We want to already have done these things. It's not actually the amount of time that gets us, but the number of things we have to keep track of in our minds. When people in labs are asked to do too many things at once, they show increased tension, diminished perceived control, and physical discomfort.

Some historians, however, question whether we really even feel more time pressure than our ancestors. Maybe we just believe we do. Alexis de Tocqueville, the French commentator on life in the colonies, observed that Americans were always in a hurry.

"It is an age of nervousness . . . the growing malady of the day, the physiological feature of the age," said a *New York Tribune* editorial. "Nowhere are the rush and hurry and overstrain of life more marked than in this much-achieving Nation . . . Inventions, discoveries, achievements of science all add to the sum of that which is to be learned, and widen the field in which there is work to be done. If knowledge has increased, we should take more time for acquiring it . . . For it would be a sorry ending of this splendid age of learning and of labor to be known as an age of unsettled brains and shattered nerves." The article was written in 1895.

G

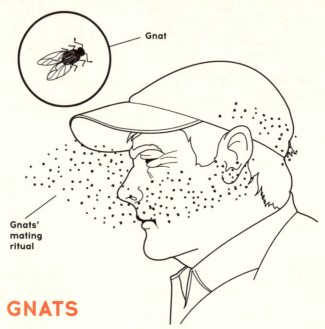

Gnat

Gnats' mating ritual

GNATS

See also *Ants, Cockroaches, Fleas, Flies, Mosquitoes.*

Gnats are the kind of insects for which the word "pest" was invented. Even the *Columbia Encyclopedia* has officially dubbed them "irritating." The word "gnat" actually describes a variety of small, two-winged insects. They're most infamous for their habit of swarming around people's faces on warm summer days. From the gnat's perspective, the swarm is something akin to a singles' bar. As part of their mating ritual, males gather en masse around a recognizable object—a bush, a pole, or a person standing in a parking lot. There they wait for their female counterparts. They are short-lived and only have a few weeks to pass on their genetic code so they are persistent. Flies, incidentally, congregate around dung for a similar reason. Animal waste is full of bacteria that baby flies (maggots) eat. It is also full of moisture that the adults can drink. Thus, male and female flies meet and mate near dung because it's the perfect spot to lay their eggs.

H

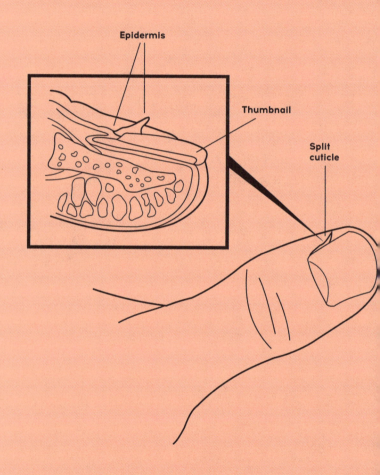

Epidermis

Thumbnail

Split
cuticle

HANGNAILS

See also *Paper Cuts*.

They aren't nails and they don't hang. A hangnail is actually a split cuticle. The little bit of jutting skin can peel away from the finger leaving the red, raw skin underneath exposed. They hurt. That's how they got their name. It comes from the Anglo-Saxon *ang* meaning "painful" and *naegl* meaning "nail." Thus, a pain near the nail. Where the "H" came from is anyone's guess.

H

The cuticle splits because the skin gets too dry or, on occasion, because of a bad manicure. People may joke about someone crying over a hangnail, but they are much more painful than it seems they should be. Your fingertips are a sense organ—they are the part you most frequently use to reach out and touch something. Therefore, they are full of sensitive nerve endings as well as tiny blood vessels. When you're injured there, the nerves fire like mad. What is more, a hangnail can cause something more serious—paronychia, one of the most common hand infections. If a germ known as Staphylococcus aureus gets into the torn skin, it can cause an infection with swelling, tenderness, and more pain. As tempted as you may be to peel away that little bit of skin, don't. You're likely to tear the skin even more and open it up to a number of nasty organisms.

Instead, soak hangnails in warm water for about ten minutes twice a day. Use manicure scissors to trim off any sharp, dried skin around the edge of the nail. Then rub petroleum jelly over and around the nail and leave it on overnight. The goo will trap moisture and soften the dry skin underneath.

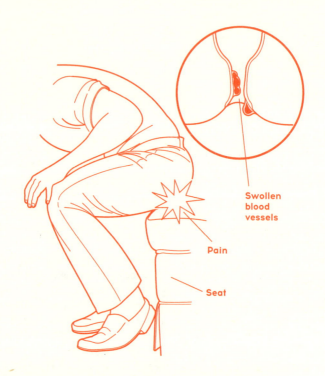

Swollen blood vessels

Pain

Seat

HEMORRHOIDS, OR THANKS, I THINK I'LL STAND

See also *Hernia Exams, Farts, Yellow Spots on Pubic Toilet Seats.*

Hemorrhoids, also known as piles or "haemorrhoids" if you're British, occur when the small anorectal veins (the ones that surround the rectum and anus) become enlarged and swollen. In other words, if you have hemorrhoids, you have varicose veins in rather embarrassing places.

The word comes from the Greek hemorrhoia meaning "a flow of blood." The way the word evolved suggests that hemorrhoids have haunted humanity since the early days of recorded history. As Dr. William S. Haubrich put it in his book *Medical Meanings*, "because the condition was frequent, the source of the bleeding was referred to, anatomically, as 'the hemorrhoidal veins.' In other words, the bleeding was named first and then the name was transferred to the source."

There are two major types of hemorrhoids—external and internal. As the name suggests, external hemorrhoids happen outside the opening of the anus. Internal hemorrhoids are found inside the rectum. The external kind are actually more painful because there is a larger nerve supply there.

Hemorrhoids are caused by pressure in the abdomen, which transmits pressure to the anorectal veins. Sitting for long periods of time can supply this kind of pressure. So can straining bowel movements when you're constipated. Hemorrhoids are common during pregnancy because of the pressure placed on the veins by the enlarged womb. Furthermore, the hormones released during pregnancy tend to relax the supporting muscles, exacerbating the problem. Meanwhile, a woman's blood supply increases during pregnancy, thus raising the pressure within her veins. Not only that, constipation is fairly common during pregnancy.

Journal of Medical Update recommends against using over-the-counter ointments to treat hemorrhoids. Many relied on "live yeast cell derivatives" as their active ingredients. The FDA banned these ingredients as ineffective in 1994, but the products, like Preparation H, reworked their formulas with other approved ingredients. According to the journal, these ingredients do not necessarily do anything for hemorrhoids. The best thing to do is to avoid constipation by getting enough dietary fiber and to keep the area clean with baby wipes or witch hazel. To relieve the pain, you may also try a sitz bath. Sit for several minutes in a few inches of water that's as hot as you can handle. It helps improve circulation. Recent studies have demonstrated that the application of nitroglycerine cream, which is commonly used for angina in heart patients, may be beneficial in relieving the pain of swollen hemorrhoids. Just don't sit down too fast.

H

HERNIA EXAMS

See also *Hemorrhoids.*

Is it really necessary to "turn your head and cough," or does the doctor just say that to distract you from what he's doing down there? The word hernia comes from the Greek, *hernos* meaning "sprout." It was so named because the unsightly bulge of a hernia resembled the bud of a plant. In inguinal hernias, the kind your doctor is checking for, protruding tissue descends along the canal that holds the spermatic cord. Some children are born with small gaps in the abdominal tissue. Other people acquire them through overexertion as in jumping, lifting heavy weight, or violent coughing. Women can also get hernias, but they are more frequent among men because of their greater physical exertions and because the canal for the spermatic cord leading through the abdominal wall is wider than the canal for the round ligament in women.

Sometimes hernias can become so large that loops of the intestine can slide through, but smaller hernias pose a greater danger because a loop of the bowel can become pinched and obstructed. Small hernias are often not detected by the patient. For the doctor to be able to feel a gap, he needs to get the patient to increase the pressure in the abdomen and cause the hernia sac to bulge outward. Coughing does the trick. It causes the abdominal muscles to contract and creates the needed pressure. Why do you have to turn your head? The doctor doesn't want you coughing in his face. The good news is that most patients only have to put up with the test once a year. In the first edition of this book, I concluded by saying, "Next time you get into a debate about the worst possible jobs, however, you might win by mentioning surrogate patients. Many medical schools now offer urogenital teaching associate programs to show students how to make patients more comfortable during the less modest exams." What I was surprised to find was that a number of readers contacted me to find out how they could get a plum gig undergoing ten to twenty prostate, hernia, rectal, breast, or pelvic exams by medical students in a single day. I am told that such positions now pay up to $75 an hour, but I am not a recruiter. Contact your local medical school if you want details.

H

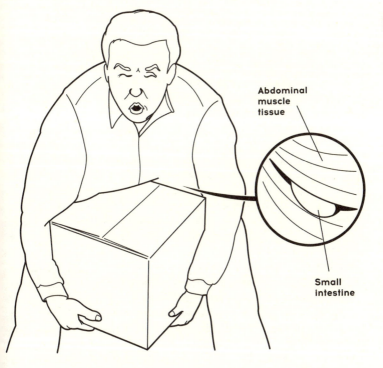

Abdominal
muscle
tissue

Small
intestine

HICCUPS

See also Coughing in the Theater.

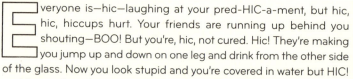

Everyone is—hic—laughing at your pred-HIC-a-ment, but hic, hic, hiccups hurt. Your friends are running up behind you shouting—BOO! But you're, hic, not cured. Hic! They're making you jump up and down on one leg and drink from the other side of the glass. Now you look stupid and you're covered in water but HIC!

Hiccups have been part of the medical literature since Hippocrates' time. In all those years, physicians haven't quite figured out what makes them happen. (They have, however, come up with an obscure medical term for them: singultus.) They don't help in digestion or anything else that doctors can recognize. They can explain the mechanics of hiccups, however. Hiccups are caused by spasms of the diaphragm. When the muscle's movements get out of rhythm you take in big gulps of air. As your lungs quickly fill, your brain tries to put a stop to it by closing the throat. The vocal cords snap shut. The rush of air creates the "hic" sound.

There hasn't been much serious study of hiccups because the phenomenon is usually very brief. One of the nation's few hiccup experts, Dr. Paul Rousseau of the Carl T. Hayden VA Medical Center in Phoenix, says that hiccups can occur in spurts of fewer than seven or more than sixty-three. They generally hit at a rate of four to sixty a minute. In extreme cases, hiccupping is more than a nuisance. Some victims of chronic persistent hiccups have suffered for decades. They have trouble holding conversations or eating anything that takes time to chew. The world record holder in hiccups, according to Guinness World Records, is Charles Osborne of Anthon, Iowa, who hiccupped from 1922 until February 1990. Rousseau came across a few cases of death by hiccup in his research. In 2000, the *Washington Times* reported that two Washington, D.C., residents were fitted with pacemakers, which delivered electrical impulses to the phrenic nerves in an effort to end years of uncontrolled hic-ing.

According to Dr. S. Gregory Hipskind, you can cure hiccups by rubbing an ice cube on your neck right around the Adam's apple. Apparently this blocks the nerve impulses that cause the diaphragm to spasm. There is some science behind some of those home remedies. Breathing into a paper bag forces a hiccupper to breathe in more carbon dioxide, which helps regulate breathing. Sipping water from the opposite side of the glass stretches the neck and stimulates the vagal nerve in the brain that helps in swallowing the breathing.

If you're looking for a more controversial hiccup cure—researchers have found some effectiveness in intercourse to orgasm, digital rectal massage, and smoking marijuana. "Honest officer, hic, I am using marijuana for medical reasons, hic."

H

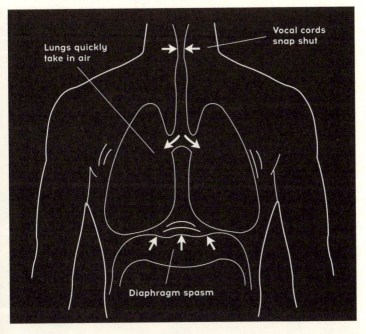

HITTING THE FUNNY BONE: IT'S NOT FUNNY!

H

It hurts when you hit the "funny bone." It's not funny at all. Not only that, it's not a bone. It's a vulnerable nerve. The ulnar nerve passes behind the humerus in the cubital tunnel, a bony passageway. The nerve controls muscles used for gripping, pinching, and fine movement. It's in charge of signaling most of the muscles in your hand with the exception of the two muscles that lift the thumb up.

A lot of sensory information passes along the ulnar nerve between these muscles and the brain. If you hit your arm just there, your brain gets overloaded with signals. You get that "amusing" tingling, pricking sensation down the whole length of the nerve to the side of the hand, followed by numbness.

Here's the "funny" part of the story: clever nineteenth-century doctors saw the connection between the odd sensation of hitting your ulnar nerve and the "humerus" and they decided the whole thing was "humorous" or "funny." Thus, funny bone. In the good old days, some Americans dubbed it "the crazy bone."

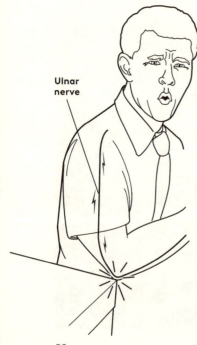

Ulnar nerve

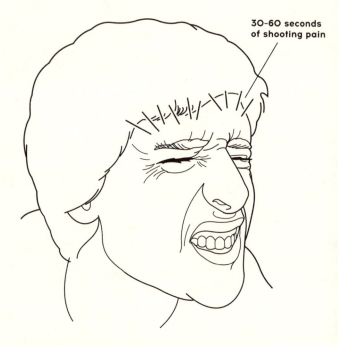

30-60 seconds
of shooting pain

ICE CREAM HEADACHE
OR "BRAIN FREEZE"

What is the most common cause of headaches? Stress? Hangovers? Poor posture? According to Joseph Hulihan of Temple University, it is ice cream. He published his findings in the *British Medical Journal* in 1997.

Whether or not you've ever had a migraine, chances are you've experienced the sensation of indulging in a mouthful of Ben and Jerry's only to be rewarded with a sharp pain in the temple. Medical researchers have a name for ice cream headache: they call it "ice cream headache." (Also Cold Stimulus Headache for the more formal among them and "sphenopalatine ganglioneuralgia" for the absurdly formal.) It turns out migraine sufferers are most susceptible to the phenomenon although studies show one out of three Americans have experienced the 30 to 60 second shooting pain of brain freeze. The cause is still a mystery, but you'll be pleased to know that scholars throughout the world are working on the problem. One of the earliest brain-freeze researchers was R. O. Smith who, in 1968, experimented on himself by moving crushed ice around in his mouth. He learned it was the back of the soft palate that was sensitive to the temperature change.

The researchers disagree on why this gives you a headache. Some theorize the pain is caused by the rapid cooling of air in the sinuses. Thomas N. Ward of the American Council for Headache Education (ACHE—honest) believes ice cold Cherry Garcia has an effect on the trigeminal nerve, associated with migraines. Merle Diamond of Chicago's Diamond Headache Clinic blames the glossopharyngeal nerve. Some studies say you're more likely to experience ice cream headache if you suffer from migraines; other studies reveal the opposite.

J. W. Sleigh, a senior lecturer at Waikato Hospital in Hamilton, New Zealand, followed up on Hulihan's report by conducting his own study using transcranial Doppler ultrasonography. He measured the speed of cerebral blood flow of three people as they ate ice cream. Two got ice cream headache, one did not. He found that blood flow decreased in the headache sufferers. "Although the brain temperature was not directly measured," he concluded, "these observations suggest that cerebral vasoconstriction causing a decrease in flow may be important in the development of an ice cream headache."

Research continues. Meanwhile, you can avoid the pain by warming the ice cream in the front of your mouth or putting your tongue against your soft palate to heat it up.

IMPROVEMENTS
THAT MAKE THINGS WORSE

See also *Buffering, Computer Virus, Trolls, Unfriended, Voicemail.*

"For the ways in which technology has not improved the quality of life press one." They are designed to make life simpler, to make business more efficient, to put an end to extraneous work. Yet nearly everyone has had an experience with a new machine that stops all work in an office for weeks and then slows it down for months while everyone learns it.

Edward Tenner, executive science and history editor of Princeton University Press, calls such things "revenge effects." His book *Why Things Bite Back: Technology and the Revenge of Unintended Consequences* argues that our failure to see things as they operate within systems often leads to unforeseen negative results.

The increasing speed of our modes of transportation has had the revenge effect of rapidly increasing the infestation of parasites, rodents, and viruses around the world. Our plush wall-to-wall carpets have had the revenge effect of dust mites and allergens. "Labor saving" appliances, like vacuum cleaners, can create more work. It is less work to vacuum than to beat a rug, but because we have a vacuum, we feel we must clean more often. Doctors wear surgical gloves to protect patients from germs, but according to the *European Journal of Surgery*, the powder applied to the gloves may cause inflammation, which increases the risk for infection as well as causing false cancer and HIV diagnoses.

Many household products designed to make the living environment cleaner and healthier fill the air with potentially toxic chemicals. New software can have revenge effects of confusion and data loss. "A machine can't appear to have a will of its own unless it is a system, not just a device," Tenner writes. "It needs parts that interact in unexpected and sometimes unstable and unwanted ways."

The Germans, always economical with language, have a single

word for revenge effects—*schlimmbesserung*, literally "worse better-
ment." Related is the Yiddish word "farpotshket." If you have ever
started out with a minor software glitch and, in the course of trying
to correct it, wound up completely unable to start your operating
system, you have a farpotshket computer. The adjective refers to
something that is all fouled up, especially through repeated failed
efforts to fix it.

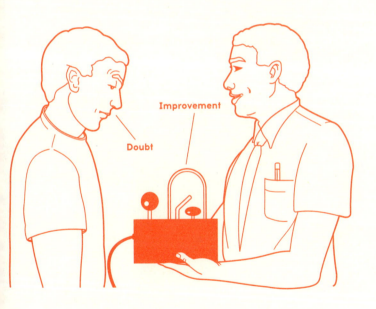

Improvement

Doubt

INEFFICIENT SIDEWALK PASS, AKA THE SIDEWALK DANCE

See also *Standing Too Close*.

You're walking down the street. A stranger is coming toward you. You dodge to the left to get out of the way, but he dodges to your left, too. So you correct to the right, just as he corrects to the right. You shift left again, and he shifts. You continue with this awkward little dance until you both plant your feet and verbally negotiate passage.

This little episode plays itself out more frequently in the lives of men than women, but we've all done the sidewalk dance at some time. We don't talk about it, but passing on the sidewalk is a complex

Eye contact

Collision course

social interaction with a set of rules and regulations. You'll never get a ticket for making an illegal pass on the sidewalk, but if you stray from the rules you will have some awkward moments or a collision.

In the United States and Canada, you are expected to acknowledge someone on the street with eye contact when you are about eight feet apart. If you spot someone you know coming your way from a distance, you look down and pretend not to see them. If you acknowledge him too soon, you're faced with the embarrassment of having to continue to recognize him for the entire length of a corridor. You must then make all kinds of smiles, gestures, and dopey expressions of recognition until you get up to the person to say "hello." By that time, you're both feeling so silly that you don't want to be recognized. When passing a stranger, you communicate your intentions nonverbally at the eight-foot mark. You make eye contact, then look at the path where you intend to walk. The other person is supposed to pick up on this and move the other way. If you miss the glance, both glance at once, or you don't communicate your intentions in time, you end up miscorrecting. Men collide more frequently than women because studies have shown two men pass at a closer distance than two women or a man and a woman. Some scholars believe men crash more often because they both refuse to yield to the other's wishes.

"Some people have tried to make hay out of this by talking about it as a dominance display, like a game of chicken," says Francis T. McAndrew, professor of psychology at Knox College and author of the book *Environmental Psychology.* "I'm told that in some countries, Mexico comes to mind as one, there's actually sort of a game that men play on the street. They pretend they don't see the other guy and wait for him to move first. If nobody moves and they crash into each other, it doesn't lead to any violence. There are the profuse apologies and everyone goes on their way, but nonetheless, it's sort of one-upmanship about who has to move first."

If you get into a sidewalk dance, avoiding eye contact can sometimes help. So does loudly announcing, "I am moving to the right!"

INTERRUPTING, OR LET ME FINISH MY SENTENCE OR YOU DIE

Don't you hate it when—excuse me I was talking—when people interrupt you while you're speaking? "It's one thing if you interrupt to say 'the building's burning down,' but if it's not an emergency situation it's very rude," says Dr. Katherine Hawkins of the Elliott School of Communications at Wichita State University. "If I have the floor in a business meeting, and I'm trying to express my point of view and you keep jumping in and negating everything I said, you might just as well have punched me. It's violating an expectation about rules of conversation."

We are all part of a speech community. As part of this community we know the unwritten rules of conversation. We give each other cues when it's time to speak or time to listen. When you're speaking and another person wants to jump in, she will incline her body forward, raise her eyebrows, and take an audible breath. She's saying, "I'm taking a breath because I'm about to say something." If you're not ready to give up the floor, you will avoid eye contact and fill up the gaps in your speech with "ums" and "uhs" to keep her from jumping in.

If you are done speaking, you will signal her by letting your voice trail off and making eye contact. You may even make a gesture in her direction. There is also something called "back channel communication." These are the grunts and noises of encouragement we make while another person is talking. We nod and insert "uh-huhs" at appropriate intervals. "This is saying, 'I'm listening. This is interesting. Keep talking,' but if you speed up the back channel communication it's like saying 'Finish your turn. Finish your turn. I want to talk,'" Hawkins says.

You might be interested to know that a pushy conversational style not only gets on the nerves of other speakers, it affects the health of the dominating speaker as well. A twenty-two-year study of 750 white, middle-class men carried out by Duke University Medical Center, ranked the subjects by their behavior characteristics including verbal competitiveness, loudness, and self-aggrandizement. They monitored them taking other health risks into account. The researchers found that those who dominate conversations were 60 percent more likely to die at an earlier age than their more deferential peers. No word on how many were beaten to death by frustrated people who wanted to get a word in edgewise.

JUNK MAIL

J

JUNK MAIL

See also *Unsolicited Bulk Email.*

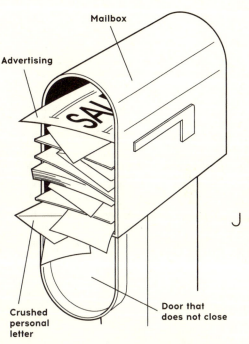

Mailbox

Advertising

Crushed personal letter

Door that does not close

J

I f you visit your local post office, you will probably see a huge trash can where the people with P.O. boxes can turn around dump most of what comes in. There's a good chance you open your mail, if you open it, over the trash as well. More than half of what the U.S. Postal Service handles is "Standard Mail" or advertising mail. We call it junk mail. It steals our time and attention, but doesn't quite make our blood boil like telemarketers or email spam." Direct mail lies somewhere in the middle of the nuisance scale," wrote Cheryl Russel in *American Demographics.* "Traditional etiquette says that it's rude to interrupt. Advertising that waits to be invited, rather than barging in, is more polite." As people have stopped sending handwritten, personal letters in exchange for email and social networking, an increasing percentage of our mail is taken up by advertising. The post office estimates that about 48 percent of the mail we receive these days consists of ads. Americans get about 84 billion pieces of junk mail each year. Direct mail advertising has become one of the Postal Service's main streams of income. Thus for the past several years, the Post Office has been working with direct marketers to increase the amount of third-class mail that comes your way. There is a way to stop it. Under a law from the 1950s that is still in effect, anyone can go to the post office and fill out a form to attach to any piece of offensive junk mail. If that sender keeps you on its list, it is subject to criminal prosecution. You can also sign up for the Direct Marketing Association's mail preference service, which will stem the tides of junk mail once DMA member companies update their records and learn you don't want to hear from them. But most people don't do this. It turns out most of us like at least some of the junk we get. What marketers have found is that we hate junk mail, but if we're interested in a particular catalog or advertisement, we don't mentally categorize it as "junk." A lot of it ends up in the dumpster, but what doesn't is highly effective. Direct mail brings in nearly $700 billion a year in sales and employs more than 10 million people. As long as it keeps working, companies will keep sending us special offers.

K

KEYBOARD CRUD

See also *Buffering, Computer Viruses*.

irst the "s" key stopped working, then the letter "d." They're stuck in place by a plaster of cracker crumbs, skin oil, and shed hairs. There may be strange new life forms evolving in there. The more time you spend at your computer, the more sticky and icky the keys can become. As more of us are trying to cram extra hours into our work day by eating lunch at our work station, keyboard crumbs become more and more common.

Keyboard crud makes your work space a little less pleasant, but is easily remedied. You don't need to buy fancy keyboard vacuums or air blowers (although you can if you like gadgets). Many keyboard problems can be avoided by covering the keyboard when it's not in use, especially if your computer is at a home that you share with children.

The crumbs that do find their way into the keyboard can be shaken out. Unplug the keyboard, hold it upside down and shake it firmly about once a week. You can clean the plastic with a soft cloth lightly moistened with cleaner. Spray the cleaner on the cloth, not directly on the keyboard. Coffee on the keyboard? Unplug it right away, turn it upside down and wait for it to dry. That is, if you take your coffee black. Cream and sugar? It's probably time to get a new keyboard, unless you enjoy the smell of sour milk.

K

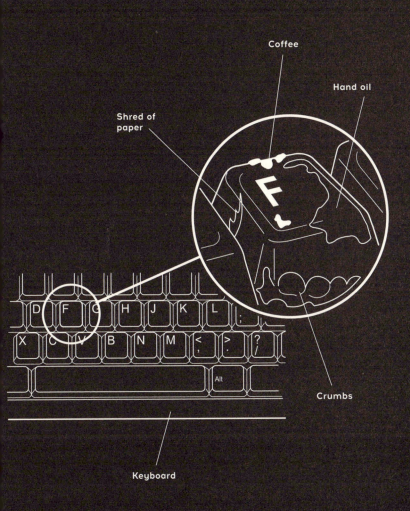

Coffee

Hand oil

Shred of
paper

F

Crumbs

D F G H J K L ;
X C V B N M < > ?
Alt

Keyboard

L

LATENESS

We all have that friend. You know the one: She promised to bring the appetizers for the dinner party, but arrives in time for dessert. If you want her to be in time for a meeting you have to lie and tell her it starts thirty minutes before it really does. Does she not value your time? Does she think she is more important than everyone else?

Scientists, it turns out, have devoted a fair amount of energy to the study of the unpunctual. According to one survey conducted in 2006, 15 to 20 percent of Americans are "consistently late." They are eternal optimists, always thinking that things will go more swiftly and efficiently than planned. Put another way, they are incapable of accurately estimating how long tasks will take. The scholarly call this "planning fallacy" and most of us have a bit of it. Research has shown that people on average underestimate how long a task will take by 40 percent. Where those of us who show up on time compensate for our faulty reasoning, the chronically late do not.

Ron Helpman, a social worker who specializes in tardiness, told *Pacific Standard*, "There's no single cause. Chronic lateness is a kind of end-product phenomena. People can have very different sorts of motives and patterns that lead them to be chronically late."

One reason is that they are easily distracted. They are trying to get ready for work, but then they start answering email, and then reading news, and pretty soon they realize they're late, and it is only then that they become motivated. Many latecomers are also champion multitaskers, or rather, they believe they are champion multitaskers but they are lying to themselves. A 2013 study from the University of Utah looked at "plychronicity"—that's what academics call multitasking—and found that those who try to multitask most frequently are, ironically, the worst at it. Many studies have shown that no one is good at mutlitasking, and it is a form of denial to believe that you are.

One thing people consistently underestimate is how long it takes to get from home to work. A 2016 study by Anna Jafarpour at the University of California at Berkeley and Hugo Spiers at University College London found that the more familiar we are with a geographic area, the more we overestimate its physical size. Interestingly, while we think the territory is larger than it is, we also underestimate how long it will take to traverse the distance. The twenty-five minute drive becomes, in the mind, a twenty minute drive. Why this should be is a mystery even to the researchers. They hypothesize that there are separate neural systems for estimating space and time to move through space. Or perhaps we judge how long it will take to go somewhere through experience, whereas we judge unfamiliar spaces through the metaphor of the map, which we process differently. In any case, some of us are better at making adjustments for this inherent faulty reasoning than others.

You would think that always suffering the stress of running in at the last minute to glares would make people change. But science tells us that even bad habits form mental pathways in the brain that reinforce behavior.

So what can you do if you are the one who keeps people waiting? One suggestion is to actually time all of your everyday tasks for a week to give yourself a realistic view of how long things take. Once you have the data you can add a buffer into your schedule and set timers to remind you to start your "getting ready to go" tasks. I'm sure the unpunctual will get right on that.

LIARS

C an you tell if someone is lying to your face? Don't be so sure. Spotting a liar is tough. In fact, in one classic study researchers pitted trained police officers against college students and had them listen to people telling two lies and two truths. Then they asked them to pick out which ones were lying. The professionals fared no better than the students. The only difference was their level of confidence. Not only were the police more sure of themselves, they became increasingly confident as the study went on.

Liars have a lot of "tells" but they are not necessarily the ones you may think. What makes them especially hard to detect is that many of them depend on a great deal on context. For example, you have probably heard that a liar cannot look you straight in the eye. This is not the case. A man who is lying to another man is just as likely to keep steady eye contact as one who is telling the truth. When a man lies to a woman he actually gazes longer than when he tells her the truth. Women always gaze longer when lying—slightly longer when looking at another woman and much longer when fibbing to a man.

Surely a liar fusses and fidgets, right? It depends. Nervousness and anxiety can make someone fidget and play with objects. How emotional a person gets over a lie depends a lot on her relationship to the other person. Lying to a person with whom you have a strong bond of trust, for example a parent or spouse, will tend to make a person more uncomfortable than lying to a stranger, thus more fidgeting. Stress can also raise the pitch of a person's voice. So if someone's voice is high or cracks he may be lying. On the other hand, liars often become more still as they focus on the details of the falsehood.

People try to give themselves psychological distance from a lie. Liars use the pronouns "I" and "me" less often. If a dating ad says "I love reading," it is more likely to be true than if it says "Currently

L

reading the complete works of Shakespeare." Liars also tend to use more negative emotion words such as "embarrassed" or "ashamed."

If you suspect someone is not telling the truth, keep an eye on his nose. When people lie, and feel guilty about it, their blood pressure goes up a bit which boosts blood flow to the tissues in the nose. They stretch and release histamines. The result is an itchy nose, much like hay fever. Your friend may have allergies or he could be a liar.

To catch someone in a lie, ask questions quickly. It is easy enough to make up one lie, but coming up with additional details is harder. Whether they seem thrown or they have a perfect answer for everything, you will have solid clues as to their truthfulness. If you ask someone what he was doing last night, he usually has to pause and think about it. A perfectly rehearsed narrative with no hesitation can tell you you're hearing a whopper.

LINES: THE OTHER ONE IS ALWAYS FASTER

You just want to get up to the cash register, but all these people are in your way. They don't deserve to get up to the register as much as you do. Waiting is aggravating, and worse still is seeing someone who got in line later pass you by. We spend a lot of time waiting around in line. The research firm Priority Management estimates we spend five years of our lives waiting. That's five years you'll never get back, and you certainly don't want to see someone else passing you up and getting that two minutes of life advantage.

MIT professor Richard C. Larson teaches a seminar on "queuing theory" and the "psychology of lines." He believes stores should always have one long line instead of several short ones. With short lines you have what he calls "slips and skips." The slips happen when somebody moves ahead of you. Skips are when you move ahead of them.

We're thrilled when we get to skip ahead, but the pleasure is outweighed by the disgust at slipping. "When somebody slips by you, your psychological cost is high," he told the *Washington Post*. "You're going to remember that." If you think this is just a case of negative thinking—think again. Chances are the line next to you really will finish first. Let's say you're at the grocery and there are five lines open. It's true that on average the lines will move at more or less the same rate over time. One will be going faster and then the coupon clipper of the year will bog things down. Another will be cruising along at record speed until the clerk shouts "price check!" All in all they tend to average out, but that probably won't help you much. It comes down to simple odds. Of the five lines, only one can be the speediest.

Therefore, you have only a one in five chance of getting into it. Even if you just consider the lanes to either side of you, you have only a one-in-three chance of being in the fastest. More often than not, then, the other guy will be asked "paper or plastic" before you.

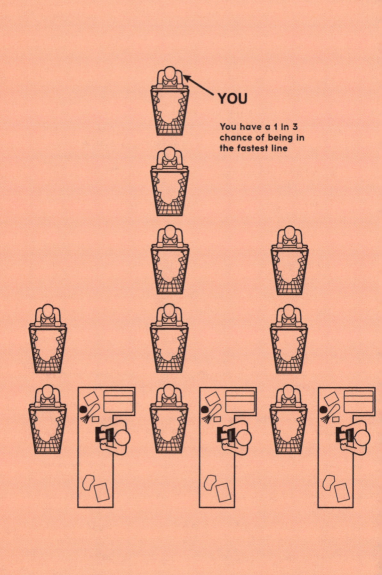

YOU

You have a 1 in 3 chance of being in the fastest line

One other fact to keep in mind when waiting in line—let's say you're at the department of motor vehicles to renew your driver's license along with half of the people in the state. As you wait in line, you get more and more impatient and aggravated. When you get to the front of the line you snap, "I've been waiting in line for an hour!" The clerk snaps back at you, "No you haven't—this line is only 15 minutes long!" Guess what? You're both wrong. A classic 1989 study "Misperceptions of Time in Sales Transactions," published in *Advances in Consumer Research* found that 77 percent of customers overestimate the amount of time they spend waiting, and 84 percent of employees underestimate it.

L

MIMES ▶ MOTION SICKNESS

M

MIMES

Entertainment Weekly once asked celebrities about the worst jobs they ever had. Robin Williams needed no time to come up with his answer. He once worked as a mime in New York City.

"Kids would try to kick you," he said. "But the scariest people were the rich older ladies . . . they would very dryly say, 'Get the [explicative] away from me.' I would get Vuitton bags in the face."

A complex mix of social and psychological factors come into play when we're confronted with a guy in white face paint walking against the wind inside an invisible box. We're affected by xenophobia (it's a French thing), class consciousness, a feeling of a loss of power, and our childhood fear of clowns. All of this translates into anger and even violent fantasies. (How often are professional mimes asked, "If I shoot you, should I use a silencer?")

Fear of clowns is common enough to warrant its own name coulrophobia. Psychologists say people love and hate clowns and mimes for the same reason—the mask that hides the real features and allows a person to behave unpredictably. Will he jump into the audience and make fun of you? He might. When he is performing, he is in control. That means you are not.

Some people hate clowns because of traumatic childhood experiences. They remember being confronted with a big, painted person with purple hair and humongous feet and running in terror.

Exaggerated facial expression of surprise

M

"Kids can't quite process it," Jerilyn Ross, director of the Ross Center for Anxiety and Related Disorders, told the *Washington Post.* "They know it's a person, but it doesn't look like one. It's disorienting for them."

People who are bothered by clowns, however, are not as vocal as mime haters. This has to do with the history of modern mime. The French combined mime with ballet and elevated it to the status of high art. Americans are naturally suspicious of anything that reeks of high culture, especially if they fail to understand it. We also have stereotypes about the French, whom we suspect are looking down their noses at us. While the average American can easily avoid opera, ballet, and art galleries, mimes often perform in parks and public places. We're not looking for art at that moment. So what we see is a person in disguise as a very pale Frenchman, who could speak but probably believes himself to be above it, who might start making fun of us at any moment . . . Where's that silencer when you need it?

M

MOSQUITOES

See also *Ants, Cockroaches, Fleas, Flies, Gnats.*

There are few things about the mosquito that are not annoying to humans. There is the buzzing, the itching welts they leave behind, and their habit of spoiling picnics and barbeques. The fact that they drink blood and in the process transmit disease goes beyond annoying to dangerous.

Mosquitoes, as it turns out, are the most formidable transmitters of disease in the animal kingdom. In various parts of the world they spread malaria, encephalitis, yellow fever, dengue, elephantiasis, the West Nile virus, Zika, and dog heartworm. Fortunately, they cannot transmit AIDS. A mosquito that bites an HIV positive individual does not hold enough of the virus to infect another person. In America, only one mosquito in one thousand carries disease organisms, which is a great relief unless you happen to be bitten by the one.

In fairness, it is only a part of the population that gives the rest of the mosquito community a bad rap. Mosquito men never bite. It is only the female who sucks blood when she needs the nutrients to develop fertile eggs. The rest of the time, both male and female mosquitoes are satisfied with sugar from plant nectar. Each time a female does snack on an animal's blood, she puts herself at risk of being swatted and killed, so she avoids the blood feast until absolutely necessary.

Humans are not even her favorite choice of host. She prefers the taste of birds, rodents, and large mammals like cows and horses. If those delicacies are unavailable, however, she is happy to snack on a person. She knows where you are because you breathe. Mosquitoes can detect carbon dioxide from up to forty miles away, according to some sources. She localizes a breathing animal by flying in a zigzag fashion across the stream of CO_2. As she approaches, she sniffs for water vapor and lactic acid that tell her that the source is an animal and not, say, a smokestack. When she gets close enough, she uses

M

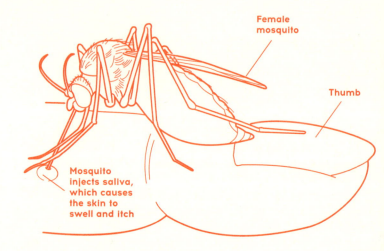

Female mosquito

Thumb

Mosquito injects saliva, which causes the skin to swell and itch

▶ M her other senses. She observes movement and detects the infrared radiation emitted by warm bodies.

She has no illusions that you will welcome her visit, so she tries her best to land in a place that is hard to swat—and consequently hard to scratch. Sometimes, though, she gives herself away with the telltale whine of her wings which beat up to 500 cycles a second. If she does manage to avoid detection, she searches the skin's surface with her stylet until she finds a capillary. Then she punctures the skin with four of her six probes. The other two are then used like a straw to slurp up the blood meal.

Her saliva keeps the blood from clotting and also serves as an anesthetic, which is important to the mosquito because it takes up to five minutes to complete her meal. The anesthetic helps her avoid detection. The swollen, itchy welts that appear after she leaves are caused by an allergic reaction to the saliva. It takes about three minutes from the time she bites you for the spot to start itching.

There is a popular myth that if you let the mosquito drink her fill she will remove the anticoagulant before she leaves and the bite will not itch. There is no truth to this, but there is at least one reason to let a mosquito finish. If she has not drank her fill she may come back. The result is two welts, not one.

If you seem to be a person who is particularly attractive to the pests, there is good news and bad news. The good news is you're not crazy, mosquitoes really do favor the taste of some individuals over others. The bad news is, you're not crazy, mosquitoes really do favor the taste of some individuals over others.

Why do they prefer certain people? Well, scientists don't know everything. So far, they are only able to prove that they do. The best way to keep mosquitoes at bay is to rid the environment of their breeding ground—standing water. The mosquito's hunting ground is about 100 to 200 feet from where she begins her life cycle. If she breeds far away, she'll bite far away, too.

Some swear that high doses of the B vitamin thiamine or garlic pills can make a person unattractive to the pests. For those who prefer to avoid commercial repellants with DEET, there are a number of natural deterrents you can try. Pennyroyal essential oil, peppermint, vanilla, bay, clove, sassafras, and cedar all have their adherents. You could try burning rosemary and sage on your next barbeque—some swear this keeps mosquitoes at bay. Some rub fresh parsley or apple cider vinegar on the skin. Another homemade bug repellant can be concocted with 1 tablespoon citronella oil, 2 cups white vinegar, 1 cup water, and 1 cup Avon Skin-So-Soft bath oil.

If none of these preparations works for you, your best bet is to figure out who among your friends is most attractive to mosquitoes and invite him to all your outdoor parties. Be sure he stands near you.

M

MOTION SICKNESS

See also *Airplane Legroom*.

Ah sailing. The fresh sea air. The lapping of the sea against the hull. The rocking back and forth and back and forth and . . . Oh no! Why is it that you can ride your bike without getting sick, but on a boat, or in the back seat of a car your stomach contents come up?

When you walk down the street you never get walk-sick. But when you're in a big vehicle, especially if you're not driving, things change. Inside an aircraft, for example, the fluid in your ears shifts as the plane rises and sinks. This signals your brain that your body is in motion. Your eyes, however, are telling a different story. They aren't perceiving a lot of movement. They tell your brain that you're in a big room sitting in an uncomfortable chair reading a magazine. This confuses the brain. The brain hates to be confused, so it sends out stress hormones like adrenaline. The stomach is especially susceptible to stress cues and it contracts. With luck you make it to the airsick bag on time.

The best way to avoid motion discomfort is to look out the window or go up on deck so your eyes will be on the same wavelength as your ears. Avoid reading in a vehicle and don't travel on an empty stomach. It increases queasiness. If you fly, choose a seat over the wing on the right side of the plane. Most flight patterns turn left, so you won't be jostled around as much if you sit on the right.

Then again, if it weren't for motion discomfort, some people would not have a hobby. In recent years collecting air sickness bags has become a thing. The idea of a plastic-lined bag came from Gilmore Tilmen Schjeldahl who offered his invention to the airlines in 1949. Initially, they were used for food storage. Northwest Orient Airlines first realized the bags could be useful in containing the stomach contents of woozy passengers. They quickly became an industry standard.

3-by-5-inch opening of air sickness bag

These days collectors treasure bags from defunct airlines, and curiosities such as bags made out of blotting paper, bags with games on the back, a bag that doubles as an envelope for a film development company, an almost transparent bag, an airline with separate business and economy class airsick bags, and even a sack that carries the curious caution: "When used, this bag may contain biohazardous waste."

A Dutch collector, Niek Vermeulen, has earned a place in the *Guinness Book of Worlds Records* for his 6,290-piece collection. You can browse the bags from the safety of your stationary office chair via the Air Sickness Bag Virtual Museum (http://www.airsicknessbags. com/). The hobby has taken off to the extent that a Ryanair executive suggested, in 2009, that they might start charging passengers for them. That would be annoying. (See *What Does It Cost? Hidden Fees*)

N

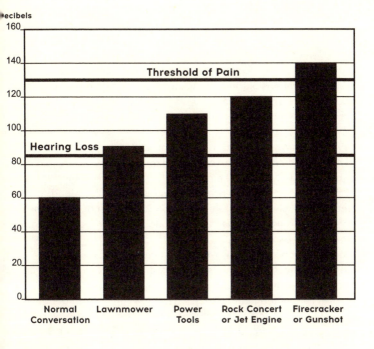

decibels

- 160
- 140 — Threshold of Pain
- 120
- 100
- 80 — Hearing Loss
- 60
- 40
- 20
- 0

Normal Conversation | Lawnmower | Power Tools | Rock Concert or Jet Engine | Firecracker or Gunshot

NOISE

See also *Car Alarms, Fingernails on the Blackboard, Off-Key Singing.*

Your neighbor loves to blast heavy metal music on his stereo. How can he stand to listen to that noise? You'd rather listen to a washing machine that is out of balance. Scientists have attempted to quantify the annoyance factor of sounds with a noise scale, NOY. The problem is that there is little agreement among research subjects as to what is sound and what is noise. Noises are usually loud, for example, but loudness alone does not make a sound annoying to all listeners. A 2013 study in the *Journal of Environmental Psychology* found that the sort of loud, continuous racket that we normally call "noise" can be experienced as a positive in the right social contexts, such as a religious festival.

Other studies have found that we're more bothered by sounds that are incomprehensible than things like speech in our own language, and that intermittent loud sounds are more bothersome that something ongoing, like traffic noise.

"Noise is a psychological phenomenon," says environmental psychologist Arline Bronzaft. The ear hears but "it's the higher senses of the brain that determine whether that sound is unwanted, unpleasant, or disturbing." Noise, it seems, is loudness plus annoyance.

What experts generally agree upon is that noise is bad for you. Hearing loss, sleep disorders, elevated blood pressure, heart disease, and psychological trauma can be brought on by exposure to noise. One of the earliest studies was conducted in New York City and found that children who live near clattering subway lines have a harder time learning. Other studies have correlated high noise areas with poor reading and math scores in school-age children. Two studies conducted near London's Heathrow Airport found that areas closest to the airport, with higher levels of noise, also had the highest rates of psychological hospital admissions. Sudden, unexpected noise causes the heart to race, blood pressure to rise, and the muscles to contract. Following a loud bang, digestion, stomach contractions, and the flow of gastric juices all stop. Appropriately enough, the word "noise" is a distant cousin of the word "nausea." Both evolved out of the Greek *nautia* and Latin *navis*, or ship. Nausea was originally used specifically to describe seasickness. Eventually, it was applied to similar discomfort on land. The related word, "noise," in Latin once was used to describe the fuss surrounding a sick person. In old French it was transformed into an expression for loud disagreement. This term came into English where it was applied to any unpleasant sound.

Researchers at Northwestern University who studied the sounds that make people cringe found that fingernails on a blackboard was, by far, the most universally annoying. What was the second most aggravating noise, according to their subjects? It was the sound of two pieces of Styrofoam rubbing together.

NON-APOLOGY APOLOGIES

"I'm sorry if you were offended."

Never mind that. Are you sorry for what you did? If your remorse is limited to regretting that there was a backlash then you are not really apologizing. Thane Rosenbaum, author of *The Myth of Moral Justice*, calls this kind of utterance "the apology of the passive aggressive."

It's never fun to admit you are not perfect. Public figures are especially prone to spectacular pratfalls for the simple reason that more people are paying attention. When they do, they are masters of so-called apologies that contain more excuses and justifications than remorse. Suddenly they speak in the passive voice, "Mistakes were made." Embedded in their apologies is an accusation against the injured parties for misunderstanding or overreacting. "We're sorry you were inconvenienced but . . ."

No. No but. If you're "sorry but" you're not sorry!

Politicians are notorious for that sort of thing, and people are finally clueing in to it. They have invented many terms for the non-apology apology. You can call it a "fauxpology," a "nopology," or the "past exonerate." A popular social media hashtag is "sorry not sorry."

Of course there were reasons you behaved as you did. If you ended up doing something that hurt someone else, they are probably not great reasons. Even if they are ("I was only racing to save a child from a burning building when I ran over your poodle"), now is not the time to bring them up. Your goal is not to save face but to express your regret. Your apology should not be about your feelings, but the feelings of the other person. See the situation from her perspective and use empathy to show you understand how your actions affected her.

Do not try to shift the blame. You end up sounding like a child pointing at another kid on the playground saying, "He did it." This is not actually an apology: "I am sorry I made you cry, but if you hadn't gotten on my case like that I wouldn't have called you that name." To apologize you need to accept full responsibility for your actions. No "ifs" or "buts."

Resist the impulse to shift into the third person. This is a place where many apologies go wrong. When you say "I'm sorry . . . you didn't understand me," you're not apologizing for your actions; you're telling the other person that you are sorry that he reacted the way he did. A real apology begins "I'm sorry I. . . ."

You're not done. Part of admitting you did wrong is offering some sort of solution to undo what you did. "I am sorry I broke your vase. Can I give you the money to replace it?" "I am sorry I hurt your feelings, I will work on my short temper so I don't do that again." "I'm sorry I forgot your birthday. Is there anything I can do to make it up to you?"

You must be sincere about changing your ways. If this is the tenth time you've said, "I'm sorry I didn't call. I will remember to do that next time," your apology will not be, nor should it be, believed.

If you've really screwed up, don't expect an apology to work like magic. Accept that it may take a while to receive the other person's forgiveness and trust. If the other person does not react the way you would like do not keep arguing the point. Simply say, "I understand. Again, I am sorry" and give her some time to cool down.

All of this runs a bit contrary to our culture, especially in Western cultures. Rosenbaum points out "[t]he conventional legal paradigm provides mostly disincentives to apologize and, in most cases, actually discourages it." Whereas in Japan, the president of an airline that has a crash will go to the homes of all of the families and ask for forgiveness.

This seems to work even in America, although we're loathe to do it. Studies have shown that when hospitals apologize for medical mistakes and offer those who were impacted by them solutions including information on how to file malpractice lawsuits, they are actually less likely to sue. People understand that human beings make mistakes, but they want others to take moral responsibility for their actions. Rosenbaum puts it this way, "One of the dirty little secrets of the legal system is that if people could simply learn how to apologize, lawyers and judges would be out of work."

N

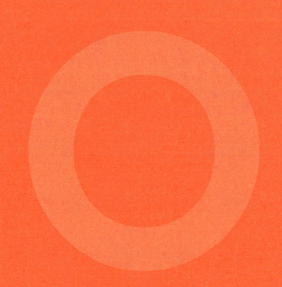

OFF-KEY SINGING

OFF-KEY SINGING

See also Car Alarms, Fingernails on the Blackboard, Noise.

I go to karaoke night to be spiritually uplifted by the beauty of song, said no one in the world, ever. Music is soothing, fun, joyous—except when Mr. Francis Off-Key takes over the mike to belt out a painful rendition of "Summer Nights" from *Grease*.

Singing is universal. Most children start to sing recognizable tunes by the time they are eighteen months old. But a small percentage of the population never really masters it. We call them "tone deaf" although that is not really an accurate description. Actual tone deafness, an inability to tell the difference between musical notes, is quite rare effecting an estimated 2.5 percent of the population. Another term for this is "amusic." François Lhermitte, who had this problem, told Oliver Sacks that when he heard music "he could say only that it was 'The Marseillaise,' or that it was not."

More common is what they call an "imitative deficit." Sean Hutchinson, who studies the neuroscience of music, found that the people he studied had no problem recognizing pitch and tone. The problem came when they tried to reproduce it with their voices. The singer hears the right note, but somehow the wires get crossed and the brain associates that sound with the wrong muscle movements in the throat. Instead of singing a C the subject will sing a B-flat. When Hutchinson played the target note for such subjects, they repeated it wrong every time, and in a consistent way. It is as if the keys on the piano were strung to the wrong hammers.

A Warsaw psychologist, Simone Dalla Bella, identified two general types of poor singers. One group, like Hutchinson's, could not hit the right note no matter how hard they tried. They knew they were not getting it right and cringed at their own attempts at "Happy Birthday" and "Jingle Bells." The second group could not carry a tune in a bucket and remained blissfully unaware of the fact. They're not competent to sing, and yet not competent enough to know they are not competent to sing. It is this group that fills the karaoke bar on a Saturday night.

There are, of course, those rare few who are able to elevate musical incompetence into an art form all its own. There is a certain je ne sais quoi that creates a William Hung (the *American Idol* reject with a record contract) or a Florence Foster Jenkins, the enthusiastic and pitch-free 1940s crooner who became the subject of a 2016 biopic starring Meryl Streep. It is impossible to put your finger on exactly what this genius is. But the right spirit, a lot of luck, great confidence, and a complete lack of self-awareness seem to help.

P

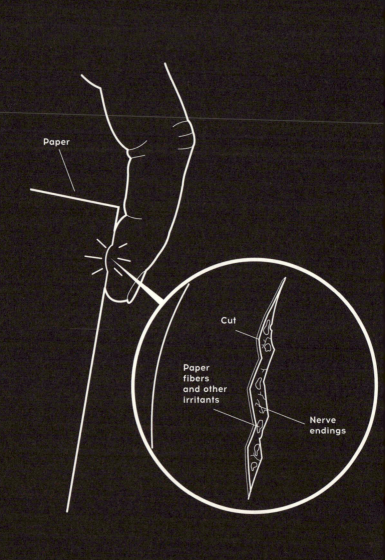

PAPER CUTS

You're handing a memo to the boss who wants everything in writing when, sliiiicccceeee . . .

It slips past your finger cutting a gouge as it goes. Why is it that when you cut yourself shaving this morning you didn't feel a thing, but a flimsy piece of paper has you wincing and sucking your finger like a baby?

A razor cuts your skin smoothly and superficially. Paper cuts actually tear through your skin. The cuts are tiny but deceptively deep. As Dr. Ted Broadway of the Ontario Medical Association explained to the *Toronto Star,* the cuts "just get into the layer of the nerve endings and irritate them. The friction of the tissue causes the nerve endings to go nuts. Every nerve is firing." The paper also contains more irritants than the razor. It leaves fibers and chemicals in the tiny wound.

Some people use superglue to seal paper cuts shut. Doctors have been using a medical-grade superglue to repair skin lacerations for some time. The stuff you find at the hardware store was not specifically designed for the purpose, so you probably should not slather it over large, deep cuts, but dermatologists say it is not likely to be toxic on something as small as a paper cut. If you do try this method, be sure you let the glue dry before you pick anything else up. You definitely don't want to end up with a throbbing, sliced finger glued to a coffee cup.

P

PARKING LOT BATTLES, OR GET OUT OF MY SPACE!

I f cities are "urban jungles," parking lots are our territorial battle grounds. As soon as we see an open spot, we claim it in the name of our Ford Explorer. Driving gets all of the glory but parking is really what cars do. Our cars are parked on average 95 percent of the time. That means we need a lot of spaces, which leads to competition and anxiety. (Like when you're coming up to what appears to be an empty space in a full parking lot only to discover there's a Smart Car wedged way up in the front so you can't see it until you're about to pull in.) Once we've bagged a prime spot, we're willing to fight anyone who tries to prevent us from possessing it. A survey by Bernice Kanner, author of *Are You Normal*, asked Americans what they would do if they arrived at a parking spot at the same time as another driver. Almost two-thirds said they would fight for it. Northeastern drivers were the most stubborn; 79 percent said they'd rather fight than give up the space, compared to 40 percent of Midwesterners. If your car is already comfortably entrenched in a space, the situation doesn't change much. Pennsylvania State University researchers Barry Ruback and Daniel Juieng conducted a study of more than 400 drivers at an Atlanta-area mall parking lot.

They reported their findings in the article "Territorial Defense in Parking Lots: Retaliation Against Waiting Drivers" in the *Journal of Applied Social Psychology*. They discovered departing drivers took 7 seconds longer to get out of a spot when someone was waiting for it than when no one was there. If the waiting driver honked, the departing driver became even pokier. The wait jumped from 32.2 seconds (with no one waiting) to 43 seconds. There are a few things you can do to reduce your parking stress. People who study such things for a living say that you're better off taking the first place you see rather than driving around looking for a prime location. It turns out that parking hunters not only waste time driving in circles, they end up on average no closer to the door. Women, incidentally, are more likely to drive around in search of the closest spot than men. Women have more parking anxiety and take more time pulling into a spot, but at least one study suggests that the world is better for it. British women, at least, are better parkers. In a study by the British car parking firm NCP, which employed a team of researchers to observe 2,500 drivers across its 700 lots, women did a better job of parking in the middle of their spots. Men, however, were more likely to say they were excellent parkers.

P

PASSWORDS, OR WHY DOES EVERY SITE HAVE ITS OWN FREAKING PASSWORD RULE?

See also Buffering, Computer Viruses, Improvements That Make Things Worse.

"Before you log in, you must select a new password."

"snoopy"

"Not enough characters. Password must include at least eight characters."

"snoopy10"

"Password must include a combination of letters and numbers and at least one capital letter."

"Aaaarrggghhh!@#%!!!"

"For security please retype password."

"What did I type? Wait!"

"Too many log in attempts—you have been locked out. Please call customer service."

Why is it that every site seems to require its own special password combination? You can't remember all those passwords. Heck, you can't even remember what type of password each site requires. Here's what you need to know about all of those password requirements: we hate them, we're annoyed when systems force us to change them, and when we do change them we do so in predictable patterns that researchers are starting to realize may make us more vulnerable to hacking, not less.

A 2015 survey, conducted by a firm that sells password management software, found that one-third of Internet users have at some point suffered from "password rage," even screaming, swearing, and crying when they can't log into a site. They rated forgetting a password more annoying than misplacing their keys or a dead cell phone battery.

Numerous studies have shown that systems that require frequent password changes only impede hackers for a short time, and that when users are annoyed by having to change their passwords they choose weaker passwords to begin with and they're more likely to write them down somewhere accessible. One survey found that the average user has 27 distinct passwords and that 37 percent of people forget a password at least once a week. By the way, research shows that one of the most common ways people select a password is to use the name of their pet, so you might check Fido and Fluffy off your list of clever codes.

Researchers at the University of North Carolina, studying the passwords of defunct accounts where students were required to change their passwords every three months, found that we're pretty predictable. We don't want to have to remember a whole new password, so we engage in what they call "transformations" such as changing the number at the end by one digit so "snoopy10" becomes

P

"snoopy11," substituting a special character for a letter so "snoopy" becomes "$noOpy," or moving the numbers from the end to the beginning so "snoopy10" becomes "10snoopy." Once they cracked one old password, it became easy to detect a pattern and find more recent passwords.

According to Lorrie Cranor, a computer science professor at Carnegie Mellon University and an expert on password usability and security, you do not need to change your password unless you have some reason to believe it might have been compromised. If you see someone looking over your shoulder—or as happened to someone I know you accidentally type it in while your computer is being projected onto a big screen in a full lecture hall—it is time to change not only that password, but all your other ones because if you're like most people, once someone knows your LinkedIn password they can guess your Facebook password and your bank password.

Of course, it doesn't matter much how hard or easy your password is if it is stored as easily decipherable plain text on a company server. As Donna Dodson, chief cyber security officer for the National Institute of Standards and Technology, told *Wired*, "Putting the burden of security on the end-user and making it more complex just doesn't work. The security has to be usable for the end-user. Otherwise they're going to find workarounds." In spite of mounting evidence that our complex password rules are not slowing hackers down, the practice persists. Why? One IT professional confessed to *Wired* that it just feels more secure and if they looked like they were watering down their security, people would protest.

PLASTIC WRAP THAT STICKS TO ITSELF

See also *Dead Pens*.

You spent fifteen minutes baking a tray of cookies to take to your church social. You put them on a plate and get out the box of plastic wrap. You spend the next twenty minutes trying to get the wrap to unroll and stick to anything but itself. Plastic wrap is also known as cling film and for good reason. It is designed to cling. The trick is to get it to stick to containers and not to your fingers.

Plastic wrap is made of a resin called polyvinyl chloride. The resin was discovered in 1933 by Ralph Wiley, an employee at Dow Chemical. Wiley had the low-level task of scrubbing the glassware in the lab and he discovered a vial coated with a substance that would not come off. The Dow researchers took an interest in the goop, and made it into a spray film to use on fighter planes to guard against corrosion from sea salt. After World War II the company looked for ways to market it to home consumers and the food wrap was born.

The wrap's clinginess comes from its electrical charge, which combines with the charge of the container. If a glass has a negative charge on its surface, for example, plastic wrap with a positive charge will stick well. The reason wraps stick so well in some cases and so poorly in others has to do with differences in electrical fields of various containers and their materials.

To win the battle with plastic wrap, store your roll in the refrigerator or freezer. When it is cold it is easier to handle and less likely to stick to itself. It will quickly warm up and return to clinging when you drape it over your delicious cookies.

POP-UP ADS

See also *Annoying Commercials, Buffering, Passwords.*

You're browsing your social network of choice when you see a link to a headline that sounds interesting. You click on it, read the first paragraph, and just as you are relaxing into the article an advertisement pops up over the text preventing you from reading until you click to close it.

Some have argued that in the Internet age, people are no longer willing to pay for content, and expect to get everything for free. This is not a fair assessment. We have always gotten media for free, paid for by advertising. Television and radio were beamed right into our homes, and you could buy a newspaper for 25 cents, far less than the cost to produce it. What has changed is not so much our willingness to pay but the ability to measure whether we look at an ad or not. In the past, there was no good way to know if those subscribers paid attention to the ads, and so marketers would sell ads based on how many papers it sold or how many people listened to the station. Clicking and page loads changed all that.

In the early days of the Internet the standard form of advertising was the banner ad, a rectangular space usually at the top of the page. People became so accustomed to the top portion of any web page being an ad that studies showed experienced Internet users' eyes did not even scan that part of the page. It was as though it didn't exist. Advertisers have no interest in wasting their money on ads no one sees. News sites responded by creating ads that pop up and draw your attention. These soon took over because they worked—they were clicked on two-to-five times as often as static banner ads. Eventually, as we got used to them, advertisers came up with increasingly intrusive ads adding streaming music and video as new broadband connections allowed. The most annoying pop up is the kind that lets you start to read and then covers the text—psych! Readers responded by inventing the ad blocker, and sites that rely on advertising responded with pop ups that block you from a site if you don't turn off your ad blocker.

If you're looking for someone to blame, the inventor of the pop-up ad is Ethan Zuckerman who performed this crime against humanity in the mid-1990s when he was a programmer for Tripod.com. The code for an ad that was separate from the page content was not created initially to make ads annoying and in-your-face. He told the *Atlantic*, "It was a way to associate an ad with a user's page without putting it directly on the page, which advertisers worried would imply an association between their brand and the page's content. Specifically, we came up with it when a major car company freaked out that they'd bought a banner ad on a page that celebrated anal sex. I wrote the code to launch the window and run an ad in it. I'm sorry. Our intentions were good."

POTHOLES, OR FASTEN YOUR SEATBELTS, WE'RE IN FOR A BUMPY RIDE

See also *Parking Lot Battles, Road Rage.*

There are some roads that seem more like amusement park rides rather than pavement. Your car rises and falls with a ferocity that threatens to puncture your tires and shake your fillings lose. One of the main causes of potholes is water. As a liquid, water seeps into little cracks in the cement. Then, on cold days, it freezes and when water freezes it expands. This makes the cracks bigger. When the ice melts and takes up less space, it leaves a gap in the concrete and bits fall in. A pothole is created.

If you want the official definition of a pothole, the FAA defines it as "usually less than 750 mm (30 inches) in diameter, bowl-shaped depressions in the pavement surface. They generally have sharp edges and vertical sides near the top of the hole." They may be small but they cause more than their share of aggravation as motorists head to their local repair shops for new tires and other costly fixes.

If freezing is a main cause of potholes, then you would expect that colder states would lead the nation in bumpy rides. Yet according to research by the national transportation research firm TRIP, the worst roads in the country are in the fairly temperate Washington D.C. It is followed by sunny California, where 51 percent of the roads are rated as poor. The two worst cities for potholes are in California. The San Francisco/Oakland area is the worst with 71 percent poor roads. It is followed by Los Angeles, with 60 percent poor roads and then by San Jose; Detroit, Michigan; and Milwaukee, Wisconsin.

Another cause of potholes is politics. It is hard for a politician to stage a photo op at the site of routine road maintenance. It is easier to do so at a ribbon cutting for a new construction project. As a result, it is new construction that tends to get the tax money. In the United States, road repair is funded primarily through taxes on gasoline.

No one likes to see the price at the pump go up, and no politician wants to be held responsible for causing that. So, as of 2015, the federal gasoline tax has remained at 1993 levels. According to the American Transportation Builder's Association, the average American driver pays about $97 per year in gasoline taxes. We spend much more—an estimated $515 per year in extra operation and maintenance costs on our vehicles.

While we're on the subject, here's a pothole trivia question: Which Beatles song was partially inspired by potholes? Answer: "A Day in the Life." John Lennon frequently took lyrical inspiration from his daily newspaper. The "4,000 holes in Blackburn, Lancashire" came from a report of the Blackburn City Council survey of road holes reported in *The Daily Mail*, January 17, 1967. The survey found that there was one-twenty-sixth of a hole in the road for each Blackburn resident.

P

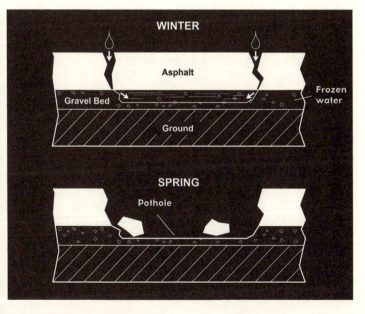

PRESBYOPIA, OR NOW WHERE DID I PUT THOSE READING GLASSES?

For most people it starts around age forty. You pick up a book or a menu and suddenly you find you can't focus on the letters. When someone holds up a piece of paper at the distance from which you would expect to be able to read it, you have to take it and hold it out as far as your arm can reach. You are suffering from middle-aged far-sightedness, or presbyopia.

It happens to the best, and the worst, of us. Did you know Adolf Hitler needed reading glasses? Probably not, because the Nazi Party censored images that showed him wearing them out of fear he would seem weak. Many people are like Hitler to the extent that they do not want to be seen in public with reading glasses dangling from a chain around their neck. Thankfully, that is all they have in common with Hitler. (We can only hope.)

A 2012 study by Israeli and U.S. scientists suggested that certain types of visual exercises might improve the vision of people with presbyopia, but their findings have not yet been tested in a randomized controlled trial, so optometrists remain skeptical. Interestingly, the formation of cataracts can sometimes allow people to read without their glasses, that is, until the cataracts obscure their vision.

The cornea of the eye focuses light through the lens and onto a membrane called the retina. Muscles around the lens relax or contract to either flatten or thicken the lens depending on whether you need to focus on something near or far. As you age, the lens becomes denser and less flexible. The process actually begins in childhood, but it takes a while for you to notice. Then suddenly it seems, sometime between ages thirty-five and forty-five, it gets to the point that the muscles have a hard time flexing the lens enough to see the small print.

Presbyopia is easily corrected with prescription or nonprescription reading glasses, the latter of which you can buy at any drug store or even the dollar store. Optometrists usually recommend the prescription kind, as they are made specifically for your eyes. Some eye doctors take a more pragmatic approach.

Reading glasses do not come with standard tracking devices. After a lifetime of not needing glasses, and then needing them only for reading, the darned things are always in another room when you need them. As readers are often misplaced and a $10 drug store pair is easier to replace than a $100 prescription pair, some doctors recommend them. One even told the *New York Times* that tall people may not need them at all because they have long arms and can hold the book father away from their eyes.

Even so, they recommend that you visit your eye doctor either way because the age at which your close-up vision starts to become problematic is also the age when other eye health issues can pop up.

PROCRASTINATION

I intended to include this subject in the first edition of this book, but I didn't get around to it. Don't blame me. Blame human psychology. Studies reveal that we're all overly optimistic when it comes to what we will have the time and inclination to do in the future. The scholars call it "present bias." That is, you imagine you will happily carry out all of the great intentions you make (but do not start) today. You want to be a person who has read the classics. You believe you will want to be that person just as much tomorrow and therefore tomorrow you will begin reading *War and Peace*.

Even though your present self would rather be playing Angry Birds, for some reason you are fairly certain that your future self will be highly motivated to finish your report, start an exercise plan, and learn Spanish.

By the time your future self becomes your present self, you will have discovered a great series of surfing dog videos that you want to alphabetize in your bookmarks and you will be intent on experimenting with a new style of napping.

Face it, you don't know your future self at all. You can track down the best time management software on the market, and read up on how to organize your to-do list. You might even buy one of the more than six hundred books on the market that promise to cure you of your procrastination—and vow to read it tomorrow. These are, in themselves, great ways to procrastinate.

None of this is likely to solve the problem because your future self will simply pass all of the tasks on that to-do list onto your future self until you are up against an immovable deadline. There will always be a more appealing shiny object vying for your attention.

To circumvent this, you need to give every task on your to do list a deadline. Tell yourself you need it done by Wednesday and vow to stick to it. Then when your Wednesday self sees the task is due, you are much less likely to insist you will do it on Thursday.

People often become overwhelmed by their to-do lists because they expect it to get finished. It won't. When you check one thing off, there will be a new thing to do. As you can't actually clear the page, you do not have to stress over that.

The purpose of a to-do list is to get the tasks out of your short-term memory so you can be more effective. Our brains are unable to hold more than five to nine things at one time. Write down "go to the post office," and don't worry about it until it's time to tackle that task and cross it off the list.

When you are more aware of the mental games you play to put off tasks, you can come up with better countermeasures. Always remember, if you don't feel like doing something today chances are you will not be any more inclined to do it tomorrow. If you really want to learn Spanish or read Proust, you might as well start now.

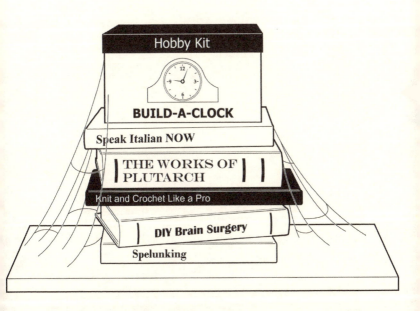

ROAD RAGE

R

ROAD RAGE AND
ROAD RUDENESS

See also *Parking Lot Battles, Slow Drivers in the Fast Lane.*

By day he's a mild-mannered CPA, well-liked by all. Get him behind the wheel and it's a different story. He rides your bumper like one of the villains on an episode of *Speed Racer*. He nearly runs you off the road and pulls into your lane with only millimeters to spare. As he passes he flashes you a one-finger salute. You half expect to see him release an oil slick as he speeds away. You could laugh it all off, but you're behind the wheel, too. Visions of shooting him off the road with laser death rays dance through your head.

Something about driving brings out the worst in people. One national study of driving behavior by a Michigan firm showed that almost 80 percent of drivers are angry most of the time while driving. Drivers said their blood boiled at everything from looking for a parking space to having to merge when a highway narrows. The majority of respondents to a 2002 survey by the National Highway Traffic Safety Administration said they had at some time in the previous year felt threatened by the behavior of other drivers. In a 2005 telephone survey conducted by ABC and the *Washington Post*, respondents rated road rage as the greatest traffic danger, three times more often than any other item on the list, including drunk driving. So we think it is a big problem. Is it? It's hard to quantify. Accident statistics only reveal what happened; they don't show the state of mind of the drivers involved. All AAA could report with certainty is that "actions typically associated with aggressive driving" were reported in 56 percent of fatal crashes from 2003 through 2007.

Researchers at Trinity College in Dublin, Ireland chalk it up to "de-individualization." That is, people see the traffic offender as a vehicle rather than as a person. Psychologists Leon James and Diane Nahl

R

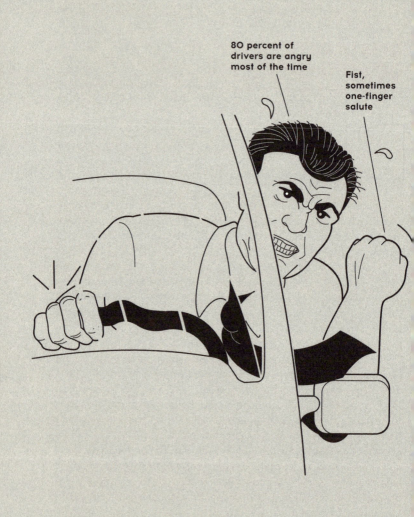

have spent two decades studying aggressive driving. "You're protected in your vehicle," Nahl said. "There's a sense of isolation—the metal dome around you and the power of the engine. It gives you a false sense of security that you can basically do whatever you want without risk."

Here's something you probably did not know: the driver of that minivan with the family member stickers on the back window is as likely to flip out on you as the driver with the "Don't Tread on Me" bumper sticker. A Colorado State University study found drivers who personalize their vehicles with bumper stickers, vanity plates, and dashboard bobble heads are more likely to lash out than others. It doesn't matter whether the content of the message was "Imagine World Peace" or truck nuts. To the research team these are all "territorial markings," and people who like to display them are more aggressive on the road.

Aggressive driving is not limited to American society. In fact, the term "road rage" was coined in England. Nor is it new. Researchers have uncovered accounts of "buggy rage" and they suspect there was probably "chariot rage" as well. Human nature being what it is, road rage will probably not disappear until cars start driving themselves. In the meantime, be careful out there.

R

▶ S

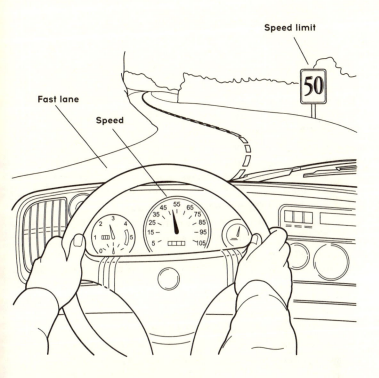

Speed limit

Fast lane

Speed

SLOW DRIVERS IN THE FAST LANE

S

See also *Parking Lot Battles, Road Rage.*

The morning commute is the setting for any number of aggravations—bottle necks, drivers who cut you off only to stop for a turn, trucks that splatter mud all over your windshield. But what do drivers hate more than anything else? According to Dr. Diane Nahl, a psychologist who specializes in our behavior on the roads, her surveys over two decades of research have revealed that the most aggravating culprit is "the passive-aggressive driver who's going the speed limit in the fast lane."

"When someone does that you feel like you're being thwarted," she says. "You're being forced to go a speed you don't want to go, and they're in your way. It's a feeling of making people be good and teaching them a lesson. It's all about making sure you're getting what you need and want. If others aren't getting what they need and want that's their problem." "Impeding the flow of traffic" by driving slowly in the passing lane is an offense in most states, but it is not highly enforced.

If you want to get the slow driver out of your way, retired New York State Trooper James M. Eagan says, the best way is to quickly flash your headlights. "Do this when you are about three to four truck lengths behind him," he writes in his book *A Speeder's Guide to Avoiding Tickets: The Essential Manual for Life in the Fast Lane*. If you wait too long, he says, the offending driver may consider you a tailgater and "punish" you by slowing down or refusing to budge. "Aggressive drivers want minimum speed limits, not maximum," wrote traffic psychology researchers Dr. Leon James and Dr. Diane Nahl in their book *Road Rage and Aggressive Driving*.

"Rushing mania is one of the most common driving obsessions . . . [It] has two complementary elements. One is an extraordinary need to avoid slowing down. The other is the consequent anger against anyone who causes a slow down."

James believes tailgating is a symptom of a larger problem—a cultural trend to respond to annoyances with anger. "People feel entitled in public places," he says. "If anyone stands in the way I have the right to be angry—maybe retaliate. Take a look at the post office, people stand in line, but what are they thinking? We've had students write down their thoughts and feelings and we get an idea that people carry on, cognitively, a constant verbal attack and criticism of others."

In any case, tailgating won't get you there any faster. Tailgaters actually get blocked in more often than other drivers because they can't anticipate problems ahead and select the best lane.

S

SNORING

He snores, you say. That doesn't really begin to describe it. Your bed partner's nose produces a rumbling that frightens small children . . . in the next time zone. A long, fierce vibration followed by a teasing pause and a tense wait. You know another snort is coming.

Sari Zayed of Davis, California, made headlines a couple of decades ago when a city noise enforcement officer issued her a $50 citation at 1:30 in the morning after a neighbor complained her snoring kept him awake at night. Zayed got the last laugh. She sued for $24,500 for stress, lost wages, and emotional strain and settled out of court for $13,500. Snorers aren't trying to keep others awake at night. Most of the time, they don't even know they snore—they are, after all, unconscious at the time. Some anthropologists have suggested that snoring is a primitive way of keeping beasts away at night. Ear, nose, and throat doctors take a different view.

When you breathe, you create a negative pressure to suck in air. When you sleep, the soft tissues in the back of your mouth and throat—the soft palate, tonsils, adenoids, and uvula (that little thing that hangs down)—relax and prevent air from flowing freely. You reflexively try to pull in air quickly, creating turbulence.

Estimates of the number of snorers in the United States range from 80 to 90 million. The tendency to snore increases with age. While only 30 percent of young people snore, 40 percent of those over forty do. Otolaryngologist Kent Wilson of the University of Minnesota at Minneapolis hung a microphone over 1,139 people as they slept and found that some snores topped 55 decibels, about the volume of rush hour traffic. Want to know if you're one of them? There are now snore tracking apps for that. Doctors take snoring seriously. The most serious form is sleep apnea, in which the sleeper actually stops breathing for periods of at least 10 seconds, hundreds of times a night. During as much as half their sleep time, patients with sleep apnea may show below-average concentrations of oxygen

S

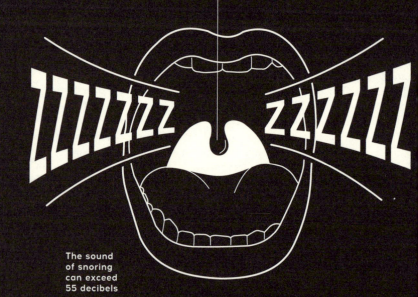

Uvula

The sound
of snoring
can exceed
55 decibels

in their blood. A lack of oxygen can cause the heart to pump harder and, over time, can contribute to high blood pressure.

During REM sleep, the brain sends out an inhibitor that basically paralyzes the body, presumably to keep you from acting out vivid dreams. When a sleep apnea sufferer's breathing is cut off, the body rouses itself with a jolt of adrenaline. Breathing resumes, the person falls back to sleep, and the whole thing starts again. These "micro-arousals" can happen as many as six hundred times a night, disrupting a snorer's sleep cycle. Studies have linked apnea-induced sleepiness to an increase in car accidents. A study by the Mayo Clinic also shows that spouses of heavy snorers lose an average of one hour's sleep a night.

People have tried to develop snoring cures as far back as the American Revolution when soldiers sewed small cannonballs into pockets on the back of the snoring-offenders' uniforms so they would not roll onto their backs. Today, more than three hundred anti-snoring devices are registered with the U.S. Patent and Trademark Office.

To reduce your nighttime noise making, doctors suggest losing weight, avoiding alcohol within three hours before you go to sleep, not sleeping on your back (some suggest attaching something bulky like a tennis ball to the inside of the back of your pajamas), and, ironically, getting enough sleep. If that doesn't work, consult a physician. There are a number of things they can try, such as breathing masks, mouthpieces, and surgery.

S

An international research project conducted by the Human Sleep Research Laboratory at the Stanford Research Institute in the United States and Ludwig-Maximilians-Universität in Munich, Germany, has taken a different approach. They don't want to know how to stop snoring, they want to know whether people's irritation with snoring has to do with the type of snore or the type of listener. They played a sample from "550 representative snoring sequences" to subjects who rated their level of annoyance on a scale from 0 to 100. They concluded that ". . . the listeners' noise sensitivity is at least equally relevant for the snoring annoyance as the snoring sound itself."

SOME ASSEMBLY REQUIRED

S

When you walked through the clean, stylish Swedish furniture store, you imagined yourself living in the perfectly decorated mini-rooms with pleasure and optimism. Then you take home a box of wooden slats, metal bolts, and a diagram. Your future begins to seem much less rosy very fast. If figuring out how to get part A into slot B has driven you to utter choice four-letter words, throw things around the room, or even threatened to derail your marriage, you are not alone.

It seems that IKEA-related complaints come up frequently in couple's therapy. "Couples tend to extrapolate from the small conflicts that arise while shopping for and building furniture that perhaps they aren't so made for one another after all," Maisie Chou Chaffin, a London-based clinical psychologist told the *Atlantic*.

There are real gender differences, and gendered cultural expectations, about the assembly of furniture. After Norway's prime minister accused IKEA of sexism for showing only men in its instruction manuals, the company responded by adding more women and arguing that, in fact, women were better at assembling their products than men were. Petra Hesser, who was then the head of IKEA's Germany division said, "A woman will neatly lay out all the screws while a man will throw them in a pile," Hesser said. "Something always goes missing."

So researchers set out to test the hypothesis and found 1) There is something to Hesser's description of how men and women approach "some assembly required" tasks and 2) Her conclusion that women do a better job was entirely wrong. A Norwegian research team asked forty men and forty women in their twenties to assemble a kitchen cart. Some people got the instructions; others only received a drawing of what the end product should look like. When they had the instructions, men and women took the same amount of time (about 23 minutes) to put the thing together, and both had equally impressive, or unimpressive, results.

Of those who had to figure things out from a drawing, there was a 20 percent difference between men and women in terms of how long it took to complete the task. The women also assembled more faulty carts with missing shelves or railings. In all, men with no instructions did about as well as the men with the instructions, finishing only a minute slower and not making enough mistakes to make the difference statistically meaningful. So Hesser was right, women do take a more systematic approach, because they need to. Men's habit of throwing the instructions aside can be a source of frustration and argument.

Studies have long identified differences in spatial ability between men and women. The science is still out, however, as to whether this is the result of nature or nurture. In a recent study, researchers had subjects from two genetically similar but culturally distinct tribes in Northeast India complete a visual puzzle. Women from the patriarchal tribe performed more slowly than the men. In the tribe where women

S

ruled, there were no gender differences in performance. In another study, women were asked to imagine that they were men when doing a mental rotation test. When they did, they performed just as well as the men did. They also did better when they were told ahead of time that women usually outperformed the men. So women's slower times and reliance on instructions might be the result of conditioning and a lack of confidence.

Of course, individual results vary, and not every man who thinks he can do a great job without the instructions actually can. As writer Jon Tevlin said, "I know from personal experience that using only pictures of men assembling IKEA furniture can lead some to believe . . . that men actually CAN assemble IKEA furniture."

The expectation that every man should be able to assemble items like furniture often creates conflict and it doesn't take a lot of tension to drive a wedge between a couple. In a 2014 study, researchers at Monmouth University and Ursinus College studied the effect of frustration on romantic feelings. They split 120 subjects into two groups. One group was given the simple, stress-free task of writing down numbers chronologically; the other group received a set of difficult math problems. When they had finished both groups were asked to make a list of compliments about their partner. The stressed group identified 15 percent fewer admirable traits in their beloveds.

The main way to avoid furniture assembly frustration, say the experts, is to go easy on yourself and allow plenty of time to get the job done. Walk away and come back if you have to. If that doesn't work, maybe you need to buy pre-assembled furniture. No one wants to have a half-assembled vanity listed as an asset in a divorce proceeding.

SONG STUCK IN YOUR HEAD, OR CEREBRUM ANNOYING REFLUX ACTION

Everyone has had the experience of having an annoyingly catchy, and often hated, song lodged firmly in the mind. The Germans use the word Ohrwurm, which translates to "earworm" or "earwig," for tunes that invade the consciousness.

The scientific literature records a few extreme cases. Dr. Judith Rapoport, who specializes in treating victims of Obsessive-Compulsive Disorder, treated a man who heard the same six fiddle notes for thirty-one years. "When he finally admitted it to his wife, she wept with joy because she had thought that he just wasn't interested in listening to her," she said. In 2000, an American man had surgery of the right lateral temporal cortex to stop the song "Owner of a Lonely Heart" by Yes from playing over and over in his mind.

Not even animals are immune. A group of scientists at the University of Sydney in Australia studied a humpback whale song from 1995 to 1998. They found that a song that was at first sung only by two males quickly spread. By the end of 1997 the entire group had adopted it.

There is, apparently, some kind of neurological underpinning in all this. Songs can be triggered by stimulating an area in the brain that processes sound patterns. When the first edition of this book came out in 2001, researchers had not devoted a great deal of serious study to earworms, but they are now working hard to fill the knowledge gap.

A 2016 study by the American Psychological Association identified the types of songs that are most apt to get lodged in the grey matter. They are usually up-tempo with easily remembered melodies and more repetition than the average pop song. The researchers collected data from 3,000 people over three years and published their results in the journal *Psychology of Aesthetics, Creativity, and the Arts*. They compiled a list of the most common offenders. Number one was Lady Gaga's "Bad Romance" followed, appropriately enough, by Kylie Minogue's "Can't Get You Out of My Head." That same year OnePoll did a survey of songs that are hardest to shake for the *Sun*. They found that the Proclaimers' "I'm Gonna Be (500 Miles)" was the catchiest song in the universe. The UK list was topped by mostly older songs like Bon Jovi's "Living on a Prayer" and The Village People's "YMCA" as well as the theme songs from *Benny Hill*, *Friends*, and *Star Wars*. This caused the authors to speculate that music today is not as catchy as it used to be. Whereas the U.S. study's top ten was Lady Gaga heavy, suggesting that the age of the songs was the result of different methodology, not the inherent melodic qualities of different decades. (Queen's "Bohemian Rhapsody" and Journey's "Don't Stop Believing" spread their tentacles into brains on both sides of the Atlantic.) The 1943 novelty song "Mairzy Dotes" is surely as hooky as the 1960s "Monkees Theme," the 1980s "Karma Chameleon," the 2000s "Who Let the Dogs Out," or the 2014 hit "Uptown Funk." Open surveys tend to find about three-quarters of people report unique songs not experienced by others. (My own frequent invaders include "Flower of Scotland" and "The Garden Song.")

But the real question is not what music gets stuck, it is how to get rid of a song that does. The only way to dislodge it, say researchers, is to distract yourself. Try solving a tricky anagram or doing a crossword puzzle. Being "cognitively engaged" can force the intrusive melody out of your active memory. The trick is to come up with something that is challenging, but not too challenging. If a problem is too hard your brain will give up, allowing space for your brain to "do the 'Time Warp' again."

S

HOW MILK BECOMES SOUR

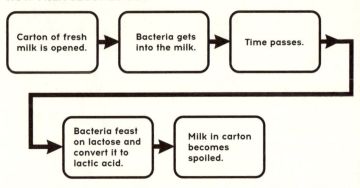

Carton of fresh milk is opened. → Bacteria gets into the milk. → Time passes. →

→ Bacteria feast on lactose and convert it to lactic acid. → Milk in carton becomes spoiled.

SOUR MILK

Nothing spoils your morning like casually pouring milk on your cereal and taking a big bite only to discover—eeewwww—the milk is off.

Sour milk is fermented milk. Milk is made up of fat, proteins, and sugars. It is actually between 12 and 13 percent solid—more solid than many vegetables. The composition of the milk is influenced by the breed and age of the specific cow and when the milk was drawn. The last milk drawn at each milking is richest in fat. The same foodstuffs that are useful to humans are a feast for bacteria.

When the milk comes out of the cow, it is actually bacteria-free. Once the air gets to it, the bacteria begin their colonization. Pasteurization—heating milk to 161°F (71.7°C) for fifteen seconds—kills the kinds of bacteria that might result in disease, but a few harmless spoilage bacteria remain behind. As long as the carton or jug remains unopened, few new bacteria can get into the liquid. Thus, an unopened container lasts longer than one that is opened. The spoilage bacteria do not do well in very low temperatures, which is why milk must be refrigerated. It should be kept at a temperature below 40°F (4°C). At that temperature, it should last about fourteen days.

During those two weeks, the spoilage bacteria feast on the milk sugar, or lactose. They convert the lactose into lactic acid through a fermentation process. When there is enough lactic acid, the milk gains that distinctive sour smell and odd taste. Skim milk tends to stay fresh longer than whole milk because whole milk has more lactose. If you have any of your grandmother's recipes, you may have a few that call for "sour milk." The acid in the sour milk reacts with baking soda to create bubbles of carbon dioxide that make baked goods rise.

Such recipes predate pasteurization. These days, milk that has had time to go sour probably has had time to attract and grow some unhealthy spoilage bacteria as well. Instead of using sour milk, substitute buttermilk in those recipes for the same effect.

Curdling of milk is caused by protein called casein. It is normally dispersed throughout the fluid of the milk. When the milk has aged as long as it apparently does in your refrigerator, the curds (solid) separate from the whey (liquid).

As for those "sell by" dates on milk—milk will not instantly expire on that day. Milk containers are stamped with a date that is fourteen days from the time the milk was pasteurized and packed. It takes about two days for milk to get from the cow to the store. There it is refrigerated at 40°F (4°C) or less. It should then last another week past the "expiration date" assuming you also keep it refrigerated.

S

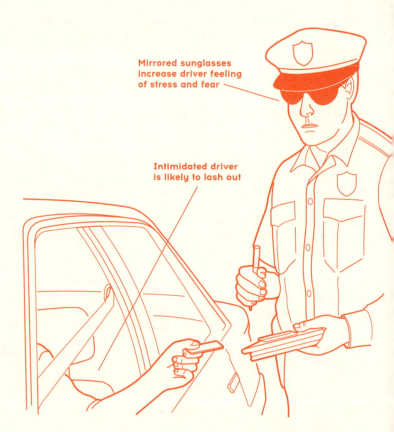

Mirrored sunglasses increase driver feeling of stress and fear

Intimidated driver is likely to lash out

One of 14.4 million speeding tickets given out in the U.S. each year

SPEEDING TICKETS

See also *Road Rage, Slow Drivers in the Fast Lane.*

Little can dampen your mood as quickly as watching the police car you zoomed past pull out of the median and turn on the blue strobe lights. Then there's the question: "Do you know how fast you were going?" Is there a right answer to that question? If you say "Yes, I was going 85," you admit you were speeding. If you say, "I was going the speed limit," you annoy the officer because you both know that's a lie. If you want to avoid getting a ticket, James M. Eagan, a retired New York State Trooper and author of the book *A Speeder's Guide to Avoiding Tickets*, suggests you put the ball back in the policeman's court. "Your best bet is to try a comment like, 'I just wasn't paying attention like I should have officer, how fast was I going?'"

Most of us are more likely to talk ourselves into tickets than out of them. To increase your chances of driving off with a warning, Eagan says you should always try to reduce the policeman's fear and feed his ego. Try to engage him in conversation so he sees you as a human being and don't do anything to challenge his authority.

The problem is that everything about a speeding stop is calculated to increase your fear and deflate your ego. A study by the Canadian Mounties has shown that if the officer is wearing mirrored sunglasses your feelings of stress and fear rise. You're likely to perceive of the cop as more aggressive and less courteous than if you could see his eyes. If he is wearing a visible holstered gun, your anger and fear rises even more. Frightened, angry drivers are more likely to mouth off or even pull out a weapon. If you want to avoid that ticket, it's your job to break the vicious cycle. Don't apologize or promise not to speed again, Eagan says; the officer lives in the same world as the rest of us and he knows just about everyone speeds. He doesn't believe you are sorry, and he doesn't believe you won't do it again.

"The members of the hierarchy do not want you to slow down," he

S

writes. "Despite their public service announcements to the contrary, they want you to speed so you can get a ticket."

And yes, there is data to back him up. In 2009 an article in the *Journal of Law and Economics* revealed that two separate studies found a small but statistically significant correlation between a drop in local government revenue and an increase in traffic citations. The bad news is, they found that once ticketing increases, it does not go back down when the government becomes more flush.

As to that age-old question, "What is the real speed limit?" Eagen says most officers will not stop a driver who is going 10 to 20 miles over the limit.

If you do get a ticket, you might try what University of California physicist Dmitri Krioukov did when he was charged with making a rolling stop at a stop sign. He wrote a paper called "The Proof of Innocence," complete with graphs and formulas. It explained, "If a car stops at a stop sign, an observer, e.g., a police officer, located at a certain distance perpendicular to the car trajectory, must have an illusion that the car does not stop, if the following three conditions are satisfied: (1) The observer measures not the linear but angular speed of the car; (2) The car decelerates and subsequently accelerates relatively fast; and (3) There is a short-time obstruction of the observer's view of the car by an external object, e.g., another car, at the moment when both cars are near the stop sign." In English, "I did stop, you just didn't see it right." That is to say, again as Krioukov put it: the police officer was not lying, it was just that his "perception of reality did not properly reflect reality." This worked for Krioukov. Your results may vary.

SPOILERS

See also *Annoying Commercials, Buffering.*

You had a late meeting last night so you DVR-ed the final episode of a series you've been watching obsessively. You went to bed imagining how much you would enjoy the big TV moment. In the morning you make your coffee (and spill some of it after eight steps), you pick up your smartphone to check in with your friends, and the first status update is how surprised your best friend was by the way the producers killed off your favorite character. You curse your best friend.

There are more ways than ever now for plots to be spoiled, which leads to another annoyance, constant "spoiler alerts." In the old days, before recording devices, the only way to give a story away was to go to the theater or read a book first and then blurt the story out in person. It did happen, however, and it was annoying. An example from my youth (when we had betamax tapes) was when our English teacher assigned us Harper Lee's *To Kill a Mockingbird.* Warning: This anecdote contains spoilers. We had a suitable period of time in which to read the book, but one enterprising student plowed through in one night. The teacher asked him, "Were you surprised when Boo Radley saved Jem and Scout?" The entire class room groaned.

S

Promoters can spoil a movie or television show before it is even released by including too much information in the trailer. Studios don't wait around long to see if a movie is a hit or a bomb. If it doesn't do big box office numbers the first weekend, it's headed straight to a streaming service. So they start promoting the films earlier and earlier with thrill ride trailers. They're called "trailers," by the way, because in the old days they used to play them after the feature film. Now they're up front where there is more of a captive audience. Some critics say the tell-all previews are part of a Hollywood trend away from subtlety. The studios, the argument goes, believe you won't go to a movie unless everything is spelled out for you.

"Today, if I had to cut the trailer for *Citizen Kane*, they would probably make me explain what Rosebud is," said one editor. "But by that point they'd probably have changed Rosebud to Jen because the name Rosebud didn't test well among women 18 to 34."

Here is the twist: the studio is probably right. We complain a lot about spoilers, but the only study done on them to date found that knowing the ending of a story in advance actually enhanced readers' enjoyment. Nicholas Christenfeld and Jonathan Leavitt, researchers from the University of California at San Diego, had subjects read twelve short stories. There were mysteries, literary stories, and stories with ironic plot twists. For some of the subjects, the ending was revealed in introductory text before the story began ("In this classic story in which the butler did it," for example). The others did not have a similar introduction. Then they asked the readers how much they enjoyed the story. In every case, the readers with the spoiled versions enjoyed them more. They hypothesize that knowing the ending in advance allows readers to focus on the details and not be distracted by wondering how it is going to turn out.

Of course, the readers in the study were given stories they were not already invested in. They had no previous expectations of how much they would enjoy the story. When you're a *Star Wars* fan waiting for the next installment, or you're obsessed with *Game of Thrones* or binge watching old episodes of *Downton Abbey*, much of the pleasure comes from imagining how you will feel as the next episode unfolds and your characters go on new adventures. "An unwanted spoiler does take something away," wrote *Time*'s TV critic James Poniewozik, "but not, I think, the pleasure of actually reading or watching a story. Rather, it takes away from the anticipation before watching it— wondering who dies, whether they'll get off the Island." So science be damned. I haven't watched the last season of *Orange Is the New Black* yet. Don't give the plot away.

S

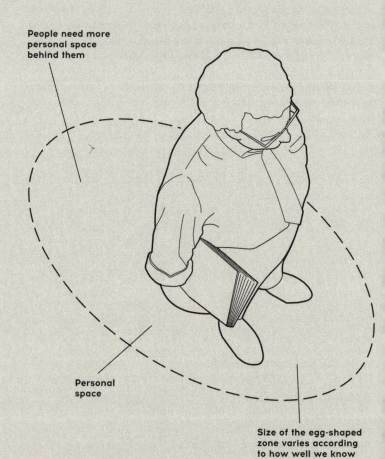

People need more
personal space
behind them

Personal
space

Size of the egg-shaped
zone varies according
to how well we know
the person or people

STANDING TOO CLOSE

See also *Airplane Legroom, Armrest Wars,*
Inefficient Sidewalk Pass, Too Much Perfume.

You're in a public place and a strange woman comes up to you and engages you in conversation. As she speaks, you become nervous and stiff. She is standing about a step closer than you want her to be. You try to back away without being obvious, and a strange dance begins. During the course of the conversation you move halfway across the room, but she always ends up just a little bit closer than you want her to be. By all accounts, she is trying to be pleasant and social, and yet you can't wait for her to go away. Why? She has invaded your personal space.

According to Edward T. Hall, a pioneering researcher in the field of proxemics—the study of our use of space—we set our boundaries by the time we reach the age of twelve. Different cultures have different boundaries, but no culture is without its own sense of space. Every person, indeed, every animal, is surrounded by an invisible egg-shaped field. The reason it is not a circle is that we will let people come in closer from the front than from behind.

In American culture there are four distinctive spatial zones. The closest extends outward about 18 inches. Only those who are the most intimate, lovers or parents with children, are allowed within the boundary. The next zone, reserved for close friends, extends from 18 inches to 4 feet. Coworkers and casual acquaintances are expected to remain at a distance of 4 feet to 10 feet. Strangers are permitted from 10 to 25 feet. In American culture, the distance between an audience and a podium is generally about 30 feet. When we encounter people with a different sense of personal space, such as people who were raised in different cultures, it makes us uncomfortable, irritable, and, in extreme cases, physically ill.

When most people lived in rural areas or on farms, personal space was not a pressing issue. It has been estimated that in medieval

S

times the average person saw one hundred other people in the course of a lifetime. As the Industrial Revolution swept the world and crowded people into cities, we developed a variety of methods of coping with the constant infringement on our space. We have a set of unwritten rules about how close to stand and when to acknowledge others. We create boundaries by placing coats or books on the seat beside us. In elevators, we face forward and rarely make eye contact. Even though no one taught you in so many words, as a North American or Northern European, you know that you can ignore a person standing 10 feet away, but once he gets to 8 feet, it is time to smile or say hello.

When space is limited, we try to preserve an internal sense of space by shutting ourselves off from others. If we cannot get the people out of our space, we do our best to pretend they are not people. This is easily observed in commuter trains, subways, and airplanes. The legal capacity of a New York subway train allows 20 cubic feet of space per person, but the passengers have to stand or sit closer to each other when using handrails. The Tokyo subway crowds passengers into 5 cubic feet or less.

Passengers try to create their own space by reading books or magazines or looking out the window. If they can't, they will often look down toward their feet and generally avoid eye contact with the people in the surrounding seats. The exercise is stressful and exhausting. Researchers have found that after an hour's ride on a crowded Japanese commuter train, it takes about an hour and a half for a commuter to completely get over the strain and fatigue.

Robert Sommer, a psychologist at the University of California at Davis, wrote an entire book, *Personal Space,* on how people react when we break such rules. He conducted his research by going into libraries and sitting too close to people.

"They begin by tapping their toes," he says. "They pull at their hair. They get completely rigid. It may not trigger a full-blown schizophrenic episode, but it's clearly not good for your health."

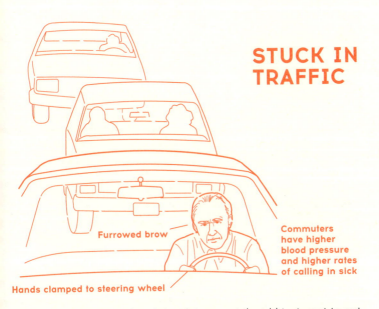

STUCK IN TRAFFIC

Furrowed brow

Commuters have higher blood pressure and higher rates of calling in sick

Hands clamped to steering wheel

"I just want to get there! Just let me get there! I just want to get off this road!"

By the time we get to work, our blood pressure is up, we're too tired and irritated to function well, and we're more easily frustrated. A 2016 report from research group TRIP determined that while the nation's interstate highway system only has about 2.5 percent of the miles of lanes nationwide, it carries 25 percent of traffic. Since 2000, traffic has grown at twice the rate of the construction of new lanes. The Texas A&M Transportation Institute, meanwhile, determined that U.S. commuters lose an average of 42 hours per year to traffic delays. If you have the misfortune of traveling on one of the nation's ten most gridlocked roads, the number doubles to 84 hours. That's three-and-a-half days per year of sitting in traffic jams. And no, we don't like that.

Rush hour traffic is largely an urban problem, so it is no surprise that New York invented "gridlock." The term came into common use during a transit workers strike in 1980. It sent so many commuters out in their cars that Manhattan's street grid was paralyzed—locked, i.e., for one car to move one car length in downtown Manhattan, one car had to exit the island uptown.

Raymond Novaco, a professor of psychology at the University of California at Irvine, studies the negative effects of commuting. "Regardless of age, income, race, or social position, red lights and crowded freeways make us frustrated," Novaco told *Prevention* magazine. "We found that the longer the commute, the higher the blood pressure." Novaco's team also found that those with long commutes had more work absences due to colds or flu. Plus, long commutes create more pollution, which contributes to all our respiratory distress. About 40 percent of smog is due to auto emissions.

None of this is all that surprising, but did you know that there is a correlation between long commutes and divorce? Researchers at Umeå University in Sweden studied couples and found that when one partner's commute was more than forty-five minutes they were 40 percent more likely to get divorced. The scholars blamed stress and anxiety for the conflicts. The silver lining is that if you manage to stick it out for five years, the divorce rate for commuters falls to only one percent higher than that of homebodies.

If you want a happy life, you're better off taking a job that pays less and has a short commute says a team from the University of Basel in Switzerland. They found that the aggravation of having a long commute outweighed any happiness a higher salary might bring.

Is there anything you can do to make it better? Science suggests the answer might be a slow jam. Stephen Fairclough, PhD, a professor of psychophysiology at Liverpool John Moores University in England, had subjects drive a course in a simulator and frustrated their attempts to arrive at their destination on time with virtual traffic. The background music in the car had an impact on their stress levels. Fairclough found that the people who listened to no music or to high-tempo "aggressive music" had elevated blood pressure. Those who listened to soothing or sad music, what he described as "low activation," did not.

TEEN ANGST ▶ TROLLS

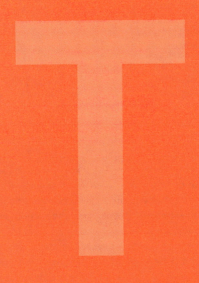

T

TEEN ANGST

"**Y**ou're ruining my life!"

The teen years are inevitably a time of angst, arguments, and utter turmoil, right? Not so fast. There is no reason it has to be that way. In fact, it may be our belief that the teen years are a time of angst that causes us to experience it. So don't begin with the idea that you are in for a bumpy ride. Lots of parents get along great with their teens, and their children are generally happy and well adjusted.

Don't believe me? Ask the psychologists. Most studies indicate that only about 20 percent of adolescents undergo pronounced turmoil and the ones who do are for the most part adolescents with clear-cut psychological problems or who come from disrupted family backgrounds.

The idea that your teen is one step away from becoming a juvenile delinquent and that he will hate you from ages twelve to seventeen is thoroughly Western. In Japan and China, where they do not have such an expectation, the teenage years usually pass without incident. In Japan, 80 to 90 percent of teens describe their home lives as "fun" or "pleasant" and report positive relations with their parents. The same can be said of families in India, sub-Saharan Africa, Southeast Asia, and much of the Arab world. This doesn't mean that you should move to Tanzania for the sake of family harmony. The point here is that there is nothing inevitable about the growing pains of this age.

One theory as to why Western cultures report more angst (besides our insistence on looking for it) is that in most non-Western cultures, teenagers are treated more like maturing adults and given adult responsibilities. In the West, where we see the teen years as an extension of childhood and expect young people to be nurtured and protected, they may be more likely to rebel against parental restrictions.

A common mistake among parents of teenagers, according to Anthony E. Wolf, a clinical psychologist and the author of many books on parenting adolescents, is to assume the role of wise teacher and to try to dispense a lifetime of knowledge at every opportunity. One reason your teenager may appear to become sullen and withdrawn could be that you are not actually listening to him when he speaks. You may think that you are, but pay close attention to your side of the conversation. Does it go like this?

Your teenager says, "This guy in my math class came out as gay the other day."

"You know there is nothing wrong with being gay, right? You know your father and I would always love you even if you were gay."

"Jeez, mom. I was just talking about something that happened in school." This is when he stops talking.

By lecturing instead of listening you have shut your child down. Wolf's advice on having a good relationship with your teenagers? "Shut up." If you genuinely feel you must comment, the best strategy is to wait until a separate time, or at least until the conversation tapers off.

The belief that the teen years are bound to be full of stress can actually cause problems. It might lead you to dismiss a real problem as a "passing phase" or a normal part of growing up. If you continue to have good communication with your kids during the teen years you will be better equipped to recognize the signs of real problems like clinical depression if they do arise.

TELEMARKETING

The phone rings in the middle of dinner. "Hello?" A moment passes. You hear a cacophony of voices in the background. "Hello?" You repeat. "Hello Mr. Smith, I'm calling regarding your Citibank card. Because you are such a valued customer . . ." No one knows exactly who first had the idea to pick up a phone and start selling. It simply evolved as a logical next step from the door-to-door salesman. A 1927 telephone sales manual published by the Bell Telephone Company of Pennsylvania touted the potential of the technology for sales: "The telephone provides the simplest, most effective, and most economical means of increasing the number of contacts between salesman and buyer. "In the early days, however, the phone was used mostly to set up in-person sales meetings. An early example of the phrase "Your call is important to us" is associated with in-person meetings in a 1964 notice from an Indiana newspaper: "McGill Manufacturing has an interesting and most helpful fold-over brochure . . . Inside the fold under the words 'your call is important to us' is a wealth of information on the best times to call on executives . . ."

Telemarketing as we know it today really took off in the late 1970s and early 1980s. In the decades that followed, technology revolutionized the annoying art. Thanks to computer technology, telemarketing has become highly efficient, and highly profitable. Most telemarketing organizations now use predictive dialing systems. With predictive dialing, a computer places the call. If the line is busy or if no one picks up, it dials another number. If you do pick up, it connects the call to an operator. This is why you often hear a telltale delay when you pick up the phone. (The good news is, it does give you an opportunity to hang up. If there is a delay accented by the sound of many other people talking in the background, there's good chance it's not a personal call.) If it seems you have been getting more hang-up calls than in the past, you can blame this on predictive dialing as well. The computers dial numbers even when all the operators are busy. With busy signals and non-answers, odds are that at least one operator will have completed a call (or had someone slam the phone down) by the time the machine connects. Sometimes, though, the computer dials a number, you pick up, and there are no operators available. The machine hangs up on you.

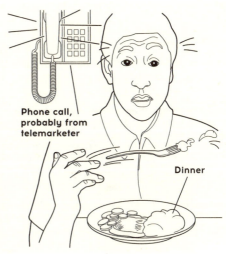

Phone call, probably from telemarketer

Dinner

Companies can set the percentage of hang-up calls a system allows; it is called the abandonment rate. The higher the rate, the more hang-ups.

The Direct Marketing Association recommends an abandonment rate of no higher than 5 percent, but some telemarketers are setting the abandonment rate as high as 40 percent. They want the phones to be constantly dialing. When operators have to dial manually, they spend only 15 minutes out of an hour selling according to a spokesperson for EIS International, which makes predictive dialing systems. With the aid of the system, they can increase talk time up to 45 minutes an hour. Productivity has been known to increase 200 to 300 percent.

So the marketers love them, but we hate them. We consider such calls an invasion of our privacy and time. In 2010, it finally seemed as though there was a solution to telemarketing: the federal Do Not Call Registry. The day it opened to the public, its website was visited 1,000 times . . . every second. By the end of the first day, 750,000 numbers had signed up, and for a while it seemed to be working.

Then voice-over Internet protocols made it easy and inexpensive to set up call centers in foreign countries beyond the reach of the U.S. authorities. Now all bets are off. We are bombarded with calls from the 425 area code trying to sell prescription drugs, or asking you to claim a cruise you've supposedly won, or leaving scary scam

T

messages about nonexistent IRS problems. The Federal Trade Commission (FTC) received about 3 million complaints in 2015 about nuisance calls.

Certainly we're not on our best behavior when dealing with telemarketers. We hang up on them. We scream at them and plot revenge against them. Businesses have found that this is especially true when the caller is based in another country and has a pronounced accent. This situation combines annoyance with anger at outsourcing.

Technology has come up with a solution to this problem as well. This author recently picked up the phone to be greeted by an overly cheery woman with an all-American Midwestern accent. There was something about the call that made me suspect she was not entirely human. "Are you a robot?" I asked. "No, I am a human being," she said, again in a way that was less than convincing. After this she began to say two things at once, and I was treated to a surreal overlapping cacophony of a sales pitch combined with an assurance that I was speaking to a real, live human being.

What happened in this case was that I was, in fact, speaking to a person, but the person was not speaking to me. They call it "voice conversion" or "agent-assisted automation technology." When I spoke, an agent in the Philippines or India responded by performing keystrokes or clicking on a screen to play back prerecorded responses. This eliminates regional accents and ensures that agents stay "on script." As an added benefit, it reduces some of the stress in the call center itself, creating a buffer between an irate customer and the person on the other end of the phone. That's when it works well. When it doesn't, someone pushes two buttons at once and the secret is revealed.

The FTC has had a hard time keeping up with all of these developments. Their latest proposal is a system that would allow people to block certain numbers, whether on their cell phones or landlines. Maybe that will do the trick.

TOAST ALWAYS LANDS BUTTER-SIDE DOWN

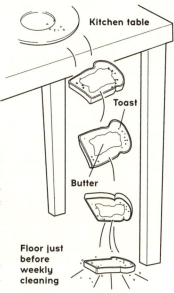

Kitchen table

Toast

Butter

Floor just before weekly cleaning

Why is it that if you drop a piece of toast, chances are, it will land butter-side down? Some scientists say this is not true. According to the makers of a BBC science program, *Q.E.D.*, the reason we believe the toast is apt to land on the buttery side is that we remember all the times it lands badly and forget the times it lands well. Physicist Robert Matthews set out to prove them wrong. "The experiments carried out by the programme were dynamically inappropriate," he wrote in the *European Journal of Physics*, "in that they consisted of people simply tossing buttered bread into the air." Matthews tested his theory by dropping pieces of buttered toast over the side of a table.

When that got "sort of messy" he switched to toast-sized pieces of wood. He discovered that toast does, in fact, tend to land butter-side down. It has nothing to do with the weight of the butter. It has to do with gravitational torque and the height of the average table.

Once the toast slides off the edge of the plate, it starts to flip, but the gravitation torque is not sufficient enough to right the toast again before it hits the floor. So, if you sense your toast is about to take a tumble, Matthews suggests giving it a swipe with your hand to increase its speed at takeoff. If you don't possess the requisite skill to save your bread in this manner, he includes a few more entertaining methods of preventing a butter-side-down mishap, including eating tiny squares of toast, buttering the underside or "tying the toast to a cat, which of course knows how to get right-side up during a fall."

TOILET SEAT LEFT UP

See also *Yellow Spots on Toilet Seats*.

You stumble into the bathroom in the middle of the night, half asleep, you sit on the toilet, only to find that your cohabitator of the masculine gender has left the seat in the upright position. You receive a rude awakening as you tumble into the bowl. Why can't he just put the darned thing down when he is finished?

Leaving the toilet seat up is, anecdotally at least, one of the main causes of minor marital spats. An unscientific poll conducted by a blog called ukBathrooms found (perhaps unsurprisingly given its focus) that poor bathroom habits were the leading cause of bickering and that it was the position of the loo seat that caused 48 percent of those tiffs. Whether or not couples actually argue a great deal about this issue, we certainly believe they do.

So what is the rule? Is he lazy and rude when he leaves it up or is the problem your assumption that toilet seat positioning is a man's job? Fortunately, an enterprising Michigan State University economist, Jay Pil Choi, used statistics to come up with a definitive answer. The equation he employed (you can find it at https://msu.edu/~choijay/etiquette.pdf) is beyond my mathematical capacity.

The underlying reasoning is this. You begin with a household shared by men and women. Women always sit on the porcelain fixture. Men sometimes sit, but they also sometimes stand. To quote a famous children's book, everyone poops. If you leave the seat up, then, either a man or a woman might have to reposition it depending on the particular call of nature. So on the surface it seems that it is most efficient, and less likely to put anyone out, if it is left down and only lifted when needed. Problem solved. But wait! We're only scratching the surface.

It seems we do not defecate and urinate in equal proportion. If you're average, you poop once a day and go pee pee seven times.

(There are detailed graphs on this in the article if you want to see them.) So the question of whether the seat should be left up or down actually varies depending on the number of standers and sitters in the household. In a house where the number of women is equal to or greater than the number of men, then the rule should be seat down. To leave it up, men need to outnumber women by a certain ratio to "minimize the aggregate costs of inconvenience."

T

FANTASTIC MOVIES TONIGHT!

DON'T MISS THESE EITHER!!

TOO MANY STREAMING SERVICES

You've had a hard day at work and you're ready to sit on the couch and watch a good movie. You fire up Netflix and scan through its listings, and scan, and scan. Why aren't there any new movies? You already binge watched *Orange Is the New Black*. So you subscribe to Hulu, Amazon, and HBO Go. With all that you're spending why can't you just have one source for your entertainment?

There was a time when you could walk into the video rental shop and walk out with just about any movie or show (assuming it had not already been checked out.) You did not have to drive to six stores. Of course, this had its drawbacks. You had to leave your house and you had to return the videos on time or risk late fees. Leaving the house is not that popular, so when Netflix came up with the idea of a DVD by mail service, it revolutionized how people rented movies. Of course, that had its own annoyances. You had to wait for a movie to show up in your mailbox, and by the time it came, you were no longer in the mood to watch it.

We can have endless streaming for $8 a month, and yet we are thwarted in our desire to have endless streaming of stuff we actually want to watch at that price. Our favorite films invariably show up on whatever service we're not subscribed to. The satirical site The Onion summed up this state of affairs with two headlines: "Netflix Instant Thinking About Adding Good Movie" and "Netflix Introduces New 'Browse Endlessly' Plan."

The experts say this is a state of affairs that is not destined to change any time soon. The reason is something media moguls call "windowing." Films go through a cycle with various interested parties seeking the exclusive right to show them. Initially, a film is only available in theaters. A few months later airlines and hotel pay-per-view services get their shot. Then about a year after a film is first released it goes to a subscription service such as HBO. HBO has paid billions of dollars for the exclusive rights to broadcast about half of the films released by major Hollywood studios. When a film is shown on the network, it gets pulled from every other source, including à la carte streaming services, although it is often available for sale on Blu Ray and DVD and via the venues that still rent movies on those media. (This is why the Netflix DVD service had a much better selection than the streaming service.)

It often takes five to seven years for a movie to get to the point that it goes to a service like Netflix, which offers a single monthly fee to stream all the content you like. As those licensing deals are already in place, there is not much the service can do about it. So Netflix, Hulu, and Amazon have been competing over long-term exclusive rights to old TV shows, which often get more popular as they age. All of these deals mean you can't subscribe to one service and feel satisfied with your selection, and no one is expecting this to change any time soon. If you want the instant gratification of having every show and film available to you at the push of a button, you will have to subscribe to multiple services, or spend a lot of time at friends' houses.

Just remember, it has only been a few decades that home video has been available at all. There was a time when you could only watch what one of three major television networks decided to broadcast at a given time and movies ran in the cinema and then disappeared. Fragmentation is annoying, but the amount of entertainment available without leaving the house is quite amazing. Focus on that while you're scrolling through all of those menu screens. Maybe it will help.

T

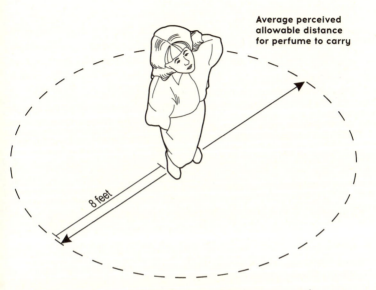

Average perceived allowable distance for perfume to carry

8 feet

TOO MUCH PERFUME: THE EMPLOYEE WITH THE SCENT CLOUD IN YOUR FACE

See also *Standing Too Close*.

Your colleague is intelligent, witty, and has a pleasant personality, but you can't stand to be anywhere near her. The gallons of cologne she bathes in make you sneeze, make your eyes water, and generally offend your nose. It's perfume to her, it's odor to you.

Your coworker's excess is an invasion of your personal space. We mentally allow a person about eight feet of space in public places. If their fragrance wafts past that line, it is now in our space. In recent years, people with offended noses have fought back by adopting scent-free policies, banning perfume and scented deodorants. These actions are most common at schools and universities. Supporters of the zones argue that the smell is not just intrusive, but dangerous to people who have multiple chemical sensitivity (MCS). Victims of the disorder have become overloaded by environmental chemicals so their immune systems overreact to them.

MCS is controversial. While some doctors specialize in its treatment, others believe it is psychosomatic, and some doubt it exists at all. The American Medical Association, the American Academy of Allergy and Immunology, the International Society of Regulatory Toxicology and Pharmacology, and the American College of Physicians don't recognize it.

The problem with scent-free zones is that they tend to ban anything that has a smell rather than focusing on the chemicals themselves, which would tend to support the idea that it is more a question of personal space invasion than a concern over allergic reactions. You perceive smell when your nose senses traces of chemicals in the air and it conveys the message to the brain. The brain lets you know if the fragrance is pleasant or unpleasant. It doesn't always correspond to the danger level of the chemical. Natural gas is odorless; newly mown grass is fragrant.

The $42 billion perfume industry produces at least one hundred new scents each year. The simplest fragrance might have up to one hundred different ingredients. More complex—and more expensive—scents can have several hundred. It is estimated that there are between 5,000 and 6,000 commercially produced fragrances in the world.

Many in the environmental movement are specific in their grievances and want only chemically synthesized perfumes banned. Certain perfume ingredients, they say, are toxic and cause cancer.

Issues of health aside, there are good reasons why you might not like a specific perfume and why you feel so strongly about it. The sensory nerves in the nose are connected to the temporal lobe of the brain where memory is stored, and are closely tied to the limbic region, which is responsible for the most basic impulses—appetite, fear, and sex. Whatever you feel about that perfume, you're going to have strong emotions about it.

In fact, scientists have recently discovered that some of the information we get from the nose does not register in the brain as smell at all but directly as emotion. Researchers from the University of Utah discovered the vermeronasal organ in humans, a pair of pits in the nostrils, signals the brain when it detects certain substances. When these organs were signaling, the subjects were not consciously aware of a smell but reported a feeling of well-being. So when you smell that perfume, you may well be reacting at a level you cannot consciously appreciate.

Scientists no longer believe there is a single human "pheromone" that drives members of the opposite sex wild. Yet scent may play a bigger role in attraction than was previously believed and, interestingly, it is related not to sex hormones but to the immune system. Whenever the body is invaded by an alien body (a virus, bacteria, an implanted organ) the immune system attaches protein identifiers to it and creates antibodies specifically designed to combat it. A segment of our DNA, the major histocompatibility complex (MHC), "remembers" this information and codes for it.

Researchers discovered that women rate the smells of men whose MHC profiles were different from their own sexier than those whose MHC codes were similar. They theorize that we sniff out mates whose immunities are different from our own so as to produce stronger, healthier babies—the kids would be born with resistance to more diseases. A study by evolutionary ecologists Manfred Milinsky and Claus Wedekind found that participants with the same MHC types tended to prefer similar scents for their own use, but disliked the idea of the smells on a partner. They concluded that people select a perfume that amplifies the natural signal produced by their immune system so it accentuates their natural odor. If you don't like your coworker's perfume, blame it on evolution.

TROLLS

"Learn how to spell before you post @#$% comments you @#$% idiot. I get so fed up with morons like you wasting everybody's time. Why don't you @#%$ and give your keyboard to someone with opposable thumbs."

Why can't we just enjoy that YouTube video or blog post without being bombarded with rude comments? Trolling has the dubious distinction of being the only aggravation in this book that is done with the express purpose of being annoying. Trolls are distinct from ordinary abrasive people who start flame wars because they're in a bad mood and someone's political post rubbed them the wrong way. Those people can ruin your day, but they did not go online to bug you. Trolls do.

So why do people log on just to be obnoxious? Research has concluded what you already guessed: they're bored. They're starved for attention. They want revenge. Also, they might be sadists. Erin Buckels and her team at the University of Manitoba found a strong correlation between people who say they enjoy trolling and personality traits that fall in what is called the Dark Tetrad: Machiavellianism, narcissism, psychopathy, and sadism. They know they are hurting others, and that is the whole point. The more negative the reaction, the more fun it is. A 2012 study at Nottingham Trent University found that trolling increases the perpetrator's self-esteem, even as it erodes that of its targets.

Most of these young men—yes, they are mostly young men— would not dream of walking up to someone in a mall or a supermarket and hurling insults. Fortunately for their antisocial pleasure, and unfortunately for the rest of us, the Internet provides what psychologists call a "disinhibition effect." That is to say, the anonymity of the online world, and not communicating face-to-face in real time, strip away social inhibitions.

Only 5.6 percent of Buckels's survey respondents actually said they enjoyed trolling, but it only takes one guest to pee in the punch bowl to make the whole thing unpotable. A Pew Research Center survey published in 2014 found that 70 percent of 18-to-24-year-old Internet users had experienced harassment, and 26 percent of women in that demographic had been stalked online. Trolls are shaping our online discourse. They stifle the voices of people who might feel vulnerable such as women and minorities. Beyond that, they subtly influence opinions and make our culture more polarized.

A team of researchers from the George Mason University Center for Climate Change Communication had people read a blog post containing a balanced discussion of the pros and cons of nano-technology. Everyone read the same article, all that changed was the content of the comments. Some of them had civil discussions others were filled with insults.

They discovered that when the comments were rude, it pushed people's emotional buttons and made them retreat to their corners ready to fight. Those who came into the study with a pre-existing favorable view of nanotechnology became even more positive and those who came in with a negative view became more negative than the participants with the less emotional comments. Fighting words make us defensive and are not conducive to a rational and nuanced exchange of ideas. News sites have been trying to combat this, but as a staffer from Jezebel put it, "It's like playing Whac-a-Mole with a sociopathic Hydra."

If you've ever been the target of the hydra, you know that the anxiety and psychological symptoms can be just as strong as they would be if someone abused you "in real life." Replying in kind only fuels them, so for now the best advice the experts can give on dealing with these vermin is summed up in the cliché "Don't feed the trolls."

T

U

UNFRIENDED

You were secretly infatuated with him all through high school, and giggled every time you talked to him in study hall. You were over the moon when he agreed to be your Facebook friend, but after a while it seemed as though you hadn't seen one of his posts in a long time. You check your list of friends and find that he is no longer listed. He has unfriended you. The nerve! Well, you decide. You never really liked him anyway, the loser.

Sometime between the first edition of this book and today "friend" became a verb. Friends have always come and gone, but thanks to social media the ebb and flow of friendship is documented. A person has to make a conscious effort to unfriend you, and even

U

though you are not notified, chances are if you are more invested in the friendship than the other person, you will, at some point, notice that your friend has absented himself from your list.

You might think that such a virtual rejection would be less painful than the old-fashioned face-to-face kind. You would be wrong. Numerous studies have shown that being dumped on a social network has all of the psychological impact of any other rejection. Neuroscience researchers have found that even minor exclusions, from mundane things like games of catch, can activate regions of the brain associated with physical pain. A 2013 study conducted at the University of Colorado Denver Business School found that 40 percent of those surveyed said they would avoid someone in real life who had unfriended them on Facebook.

Of course, not all friendships are created equal whether online or off. Most of the people in your friends list are not what you might call intimates. Anthropologists suggest that a human being is capable of maintaining no more than 150 meaningful relationships. If you have 300 Facebook friends, you've probably accepted friend requests from your mailman and a friend of a friend you met once at a party three years ago. "Friends" who are most likely to be dumped on social networks are friends from school, back when you were thrown together and hadn't developed your own likes and political opinions. (Political differences are one of the main reasons people hide or drop friends on social networks.)

There are certainly people in your list who you would not notice at all if they disappeared. You are that person on someone else's list. The problem comes, online as elsewhere in life, when your idea of your level of friendship does not match the view of the other person. There is no way around it, when a person you thought was a friend turns out to be an acquaintance or less, it hurts. But you do not have to suffer.

Psychological studies have shown that the best way to get over the pain of rejection is to stop trying to figure out what went wrong and to reconnect with people who do love you. Talking about the pain of being unfriended with your remaining friends helps.

U

UNMATCHED SOCKS

You start out with a drawer full of nice pairs of matched socks. Eventually, the order degrades to the point that you are forced to go to work wearing one argyle and one blue sock. What happened? Where the lost socks go is one of the great mysteries of the universe; but Robert Matthews, a visiting research fellow at Aston University in Birmingham, England, has investigated the results. His conclusion, published in *Mathematics Today*, is that if your socks do go missing, you are indeed more likely to end up with unmatched socks than pairs.

U

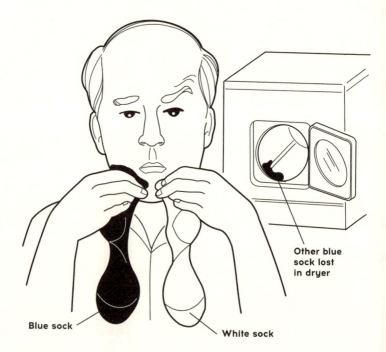

Other blue
sock lost
in dryer

Blue sock

White sock

Here's how it works: when you lose one sock, it leaves behind its former partner. If you lose another sock, it could be the unmatched one (how great would that be). But there are many more paired socks than single socks, so it is probable that the next sock you lose will not be the matchless one. Because you are less likely to wear and wash the unmatched sock, leaving it safe and sound in the drawer where it is unlikely to be lost, the odds are even greater that the next sock to go will be part of a pair. Using a series of complex sock equations, Matthews concluded that if socks are randomly lost from a drawer initially stocked with ten complete, but distinct, sock pairs, it is over one hundred times more likely that the result will be the worst possible outcome, with four complete pairs and six odd socks in the drawer, than the best outcome with seven complete pairs left.

"Drawing two socks at random even from a drawer full of complete pairs is most likely to produce nothing but two odd socks," he writes. "Thus, even if we have judiciously cleared out all the odd socks from our drawer we are still likely to have to rummage through a substantial fraction of the remaining socks before getting just one matching pair." Of course, you increase the chances of pulling out matching socks if you buy only one kind. Matthews thought that was a bit drastic. He decided to limit his own sock purchases to two types, eight pairs of each. He learned, however, that Murphy's Law cannot be broken. After the sock gremlins struck, he returned to the store only to discover that one of the styles had been discontinued.

U ◀

UNSOLICITED BULK EMAIL, AKA SPAM

Unsolicited bulk email got its nickname from a sketch on the British television program *Monty Python's Flying Circus* in which everything on the menu came with Spam. The inbox of your email program is similar—spam, spam, message from your mom, spam, business correspondence, and spam.

The folks at Hormel, makers of the canned meat product, SPAM, aren't thrilled at the association with bulk email, by the way. Yet they have pretty much given up and accepted that we're not going to change our moniker for the annoying messages. Their lawyers, instead, concentrate their energies on making sure people don't capitalize the word "spam" when referring to email and keeping pictures of the meat off of webpages about Internet spam.

The good news about spam, the electronic kind, is that it has fallen to its lowest level in more than a decade. The bad news is you're getting less spam because the "Nigerian princes" have moved on from email scams to programming malware to steal your passwords and money directly. As spam has decreased, malicious software has increased. Some of the plain old marketing spam has also moved to your social network.

We really hate spam. A study conducted by the University of Georgia in 2006 compared our annoyance with spam versus junk mail and we hate our intrusive email more than those uninvited mailers. The study's authors speculate that this is because unwanted mail doesn't seem to thwart your efforts to see new messages the way downloading unwanted email does.

There may be less of spam today, but it there is still a lot of it. Symantec reported in 2015 that 49.7 percent of the email it scans contains spam. The 100 billion spam messages sent per day is not exactly what you would call a small volume. Then there is the solicited, but not really welcome, mass of messages like subscriptions to lists

U

you haven't bothered to cancel, and social network notifications about random cat videos your acquaintances posted.

If your inbox gets on your nerves now, be grateful that we do not yet have some of the spam innovations that the experts are predicting, such as bots that are so good at mimicking human interaction that they fool you into thinking they are your friends. Or how about this nightmare scenario envisioned by Kristoffer Gansing, the artistic director of the Transmediale Festival for digital art and culture:

"With 3D-printing technology becoming more widely available, I can imagine a new kind of physical spam becoming possible," he told the *Independent*, "spamming people's workplaces and private lives with unwanted objects."

U ◀

VENDING MACHINES

V

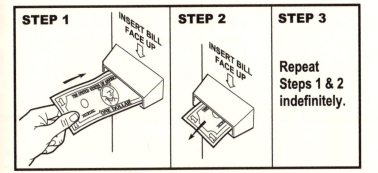

STEP 1	STEP 2	STEP 3
INSERT BILL FACE UP	INSERT BILL FACE UP	**Repeat Steps 1 & 2 indefinitely.**

VENDING MACHINES SPITTING OUT YOUR DOLLAR

A quarter doesn't go as far as it used to. Fortunately, technology has advanced to the point that machines can read paper money. Unfortunately, technology has not advanced to the point that it can always read paper money. Unless you have been living in a cave for the past twenty years, chances are you've had the experience of watching a perfectly good dollar bill slide in and out of a machine accompanied by a distinctive "zzzziipp." Why is it that one machine will accept a wrinkled dollar and another won't? As the computer people say, "It's not a bug, it's a feature."

Vending machines are designed so that their owners can make money. They can't make money if the machine is easily fooled by counterfeit cash and dollar-shaped photocopies. On the other hand, the vendor makes no money if you walk away without buying anything because the machine won't take your legal tender. So the manufacturers try to strike a balance between security and accepting mangled money. Coin Acceptors Inc. of St. Louis is one of the leading manufacturers of the devices that read bills. They offer their vendors a choice of three levels of security. Those who put their machines in

V

high traffic areas often opt for high security. A machine in an office might be safe with a lower level of security.

After a machine pulls the paper in, it scans it with light beams. The scanners are so sensitive they can tell what type of ink is used, what color it is, and what type of engravings appear. The highest level of security rejects bills with any imperfections, such as a torn corner. On the other hand, they can also be set so that they will take bills that have been slightly torn, splattered with food, soaked in water, or written on with a pen. Even the most forgiving setting, however, can be fooled by a bill that is too crumpled. The folds distort the image on the face.

Another possibility is that the machine has not been cleaned regularly and a buildup of money grime on the scanners is to blame. The best advice if a machine rejects your money is to change it in for a new bill. If you can't do that, walk away. Don't try to rock the machine to get a free candy bar—you could get seriously hurt. On average, two people are crushed to death each year by toppling vending machines.

V

W

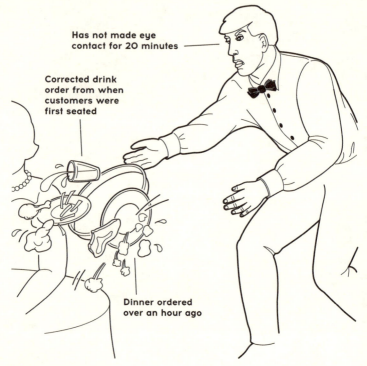

Has not made eye
contact for 20 minutes

Corrected drink
order from when
customers were
first seated

Dinner ordered
over an hour ago

WAITERS

See also *What Did I Come in Here For?*

W
ou're already fidgety and annoyed at having to wait a half
hour to get a table at Chez Bob. You even called in a
reservation. Chad, your server for this evening, leans on the
back of an empty chair as he takes your order. For a
moment, you hesitate between ordering the chicken and the fish. "I
can come back," he says, and disappears. Ten minutes later he
returns, takes your order, but comes back with the wrong drinks.
Once again he sprints away before you can call his attention to the
error. Chad steadfastly refuses to make eye contact, and although he

passes close to your table three times, he appears to have absolutely no hearing or peripheral vision.

When he brings your meals, you finally have a chance to mention your drink order. He takes your drinks away, promising to return with fresh ones. Time passes. He only returns when you are deep in conversation and interrupts you mid-sentence to ask, "How is everything this evening?" "Well, we don't have any drinks!" you snap. He rolls his eyes as if to say, "What a rude customer." By the time Chad returns with the right drinks, three out of four of your guests have finished their meals. Chad starts clearing the plates of all of them, including the one who has not finished. You decide not to risk dessert. Finally, Chad returns with the check and hands it to the only male at the table. He then disappears into a vast waitperson void as his tip dwindles from 15 percent, to 10 percent, to 5 percent . . . Finally, you take the check to the front of the restaurant and ask whom you can pay. As you leave, you hear Chad complain loudly that he got stiffed on his tip.

Has waitstaff gotten worse in the past few years? Probably. A strong economy gave us a boom in restaurants; meanwhile, employees had more options. They could pick and choose their jobs. This led to a shortage of qualified waiters and waitresses. "We joke that pretty soon the chef is going to have to yell: "'Ok, table number five, come and get your food,'" said one New Jersey restauranteur.

According to restaurant critic Tim Zagat, women get the worst restaurant service because there is an assumption that women, as a group, do not tip. There is also an assumption that a man at the table is paying. Waiters and waitresses alike tend to put the check down in front of a man, even if a woman is the hostess.

In some countries, waiting tables is considered to be a highly skilled enterprise. There are highly regarded schools in Europe to train waiters. Not so in this country. Here, waiting tables is more often seen as something students and out-of-work actors do. Restaurants don't want to invest in a great deal of training if the employees aren't going to stick around. Waiters who do take pride in their profession are valuable and rare enough that they end up at the top restaurants, not Chez Bob.

According to the National Waiters Association, a good server should check on the diner once in the first 90 seconds after the meal is put down on the table. He should then keep the diners in view and pay attention, but should not interrupt with questions like, "How is your food?" He should never clear the plates until the slowest diner is through. If the check is delivered to the table, it should be set in the center, not in front of any one diner unless requested. And of course, it should be picked up promptly.

At Chez Bob, waiters are paid less than minimum wage and they have to split their tips with the busboys, greeters, and kitchen staff. Chez Bob is always understaffed and Chad was recently hired. His previous job was washing windows. He was thrown into the deep end and always feels a little out of his element. Today, his coworker Annie called in sick and he is covering her tables as well as his own. One of the customers in her section is a regular who orders food for an invisible friend and shouts at the waiter if he doesn't bring it and set it at perfect right angles. All of his customers are annoyed to begin with because Bob insists on overbooking. Many people call in reservations, don't show up, and never call to cancel. If everyone does show up, there is not enough room for them all. That means long waits for everyone and short tempers all around. Chad is keeping track of so many little things that they often get erased from his short-term memory before he has a chance to process them. Because he is overwhelmed, he is easily irritated by things—including you. Chad does not lack peripheral vision—he is ignoring you because he isn't ready to deal with your table just yet.

And the time when waiters seem most apt to get lost?—after they bring the check. Mentally, they have stopped worrying about you because your meal is done. It's easier to forget to pick up the check and bring change than it is to ignore someone waiving his arm shouting, "Waiter! I ordered soup an hour ago!"

W

WHAT DID I COME IN HERE FOR? OR DESTINESIA

See also *What Is the Word?*

It's like there's a force field between your bedroom and living room. You get up off the couch, propelled by a desire to get something. You pass through the door and poof!, your memory is gone. What am I doing in this room? I know I came in here for something.

You are not going insane, you just have insufficient RAM at this time. Your short-term, or "working," memory, is analogous to the RAM on your computer. It is temporary storage of information you need to keep in your head while you perform tasks that require that information.

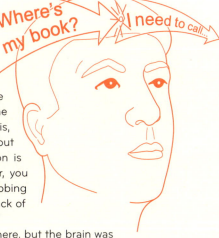

There is a lot of information out there for the brain to process. You're not aware of much of the information your senses relay to the brain. While you are reading this, you are probably not thinking about your tongue. When your attention is brought to your tongue, however, you become aware of how it feels rubbing against that rough tooth in the back of your mouth.

That information was always there, but the brain was filtering it out. More than 99 percent of the sensory information that comes in is deemed irrelevant by the brain and it is not encoded into long-term memory. Some information needs to be in your consciousness just long enough to act on it—a decision to go into another room, for example.

W

"The first law of memory, in terms of cognitive processes is that in order to remember something—encode something in the brain—you have to pay attention to it," says Dr. Sonia Lupien, a neuro-psychologist at Douglas Hospital in Montréal, Canada, who specializes in the effects of stress on memory. "Many times when we 'forget' these little things, it's not even forgetting. It's not having encoded it in the first place."

Usually we do not concentrate on one task at a time. Our attention is divided. When you were sitting on the couch contemplating a trip into the bedroom, you were also thinking about what to make for dinner, whether the kids had done their homework, and how long it would be before your favorite show came on TV.

"Because we cannot put everything into our memory, we decide what is relevant and should be encoded and what is not," Lupien says. "The more things you do at the same time, the less you are going to be able to say this one is relevant, this one is not. The probability that it doesn't even get in will explain why, when you get to the room you have no idea why you went there."

The reason older people seem to experience this more often is that many of the things their minds used to give priority to now fall into the less relevant category. "If before it was important to know where your glasses were because you had four minutes to leave the house, you unconsciously would say 'here they are. I know they are here. This is important.' However, once you retire you have all the time in the world. Unconsciously it's not as important to find your glasses in .22 seconds. So you will not process this information in the same way."

Want to be sure to remember why you went into the room? Put it higher on your list of priorities.

 W

WHAT DOES IT REALLY COST? HIDDEN FEES

People hate it when their favorite brands raise their prices. Corporations know this, so they have to come up with a way to cover rising costs, or provide increasing returns to shareholders, while making it appear that they haven't raised their prices. Increasingly, they have done this through sleight of hand by tacking on hidden fees or taking aspects of a service that were once included and setting them aside as premiums, available for an added fee. They call this "unbundling."

In January 2017, the National Economic Council released a report blasting airlines and hotels for hidden fees that drive up the costs of their products and services. "When pricing is unclear, it threatens the competitive process by which consumers make decisions," the report said. Of course, you discovered that without their help when you went to check into that $26 Las Vegas hotel room only to find that "resort fees" disclosed in the small print ran your bill up to $90. With most people carrying their own cell phones, those $2 fees to use the landline in your room have mostly disappeared. But $1.50 "safe fees" (for having a safe in your room) have become common.

The most obvious case is in the airline industry. Since the airlines do nothing much to differentiate their brands in our minds, they have all joined in a race to the bottom, first eliminating meals, then snacks, then free movies, then the little blankets, then checked bags. Instead of giving you these things, they charge you an à la carte fee after you've paid for your ticket. It generally doesn't make your flight cheaper, it just makes it seem cheaper, and hopefully it seems cheaper than the other airlines offerings. Unbundling unleashed in 2007 and airlines started to separately monetize everything that was not fuel or fuselage. This led to the Reuters headline in 2009, "U.S. Airlines Might Have Reached Limit on New Fees." But Reuters underestimated their creativity.

W

Recently airlines discovered that they had trained their customers not to check bags any more, and the "ancillary revenue" from checked bags had dropped to a dangerously low level. So some airlines started charging for carry-ons. This was followed by the practice of making the advance reservation of a seat a premium service. The Senate Commerce Committee, in 2015, after a review of seven different airline websites, found that "consumers do not generally receive prominent disclosures regarding these fees when procuring airfare." The fees are usually found in small print under headers like "fare rules," or "optional services."

The lack of amenities has created its own set of annoyances, not the least of which is not actually knowing how much your vacation will cost. There is also the fact that more people are bringing their own meals onto flights that do not provide them. This bothers the neighbors who are tied into an uncomfortably small space beside someone with a garlic and tuna sandwich. A recent survey by GO Airport Express found that almost half of respondents said it was rude to carry on food with a strong odor. So don't do that.

Airlines and hotels are not the only companies that have tacked on fees for things they once offered for free. If you get your Internet through a cable company, there is a good chance a modem rental fee of $6 or $7 a month has started to appear on your bill. Prepaid gift cards can come with a whole host of fees including swipe fees, activation fees, reloading fees, and fees for not using the card by a certain time.

Even retail products can be made to seem artificially cheaper by redesigning product packaging. The sticker price remains the same, but the amount of product you get is reduced. Have you noticed that your peanut butter jar is now dented inward at the bottom? It holds two ounces less than it used to. Boxes of breakfast cereal are the same height they've always been, and look the same on the shelf. But the depth has shrunk, decreasing the box's volume. Your toilet tissue still says it has 1,000 sheets, but the sheets have gotten a bit shorter. The old six-ounce can of tuna now holds five ounces.

Of course it does a company no good to alienate its customers. If unexpected hidden costs make us fume, why do they do it? The answer, according to Harvard professor David Laibson and Xavier Gabaix of MIT, seems to be that it only makes some of us fume, and that is good enough to keep things profitable.

They divide the consumer world into two categories: "sophisticates" and "myopes." The sophisticates are good at comparison shopping, paying attention to the fine print, and finding ways to avoid hidden fees. Myopes take advertised prices at face value and don't pay much attention to the final bill. Businesses like the latter group, because they can extract a bit of extra money from them from time to time. Now, if they were to start advertising that they treat their customers fairly, unlike their competitors who include hidden fees, they have not given the sophisticates any new information. They already did the work to find out what the lowest price is, fees and all. All they have done, therefore, is alert the myopes and transform some of them into sophisticates. Businesses don't want a bunch of sophisticates—they spend less money. If you create more sophisticates, you make people more conscious of spending everywhere, including at your hotel or airline. Thus Laibson and Gabaix conclude, "Neither firm has an incentive to do it." You're left with only two choices: become a sophisticate or expect to pay more than you expected.

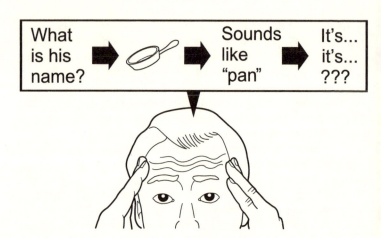

WHAT IS THE WORD?

See also *What Did I Come in Here For?*

I went to the store because I wanted . . . I had a recipe that called for . . . You know, one of those green things . . . it's not a cantaloupe. It's a vegetable, you know . . . It's . . . uurrrggghhh. It's green . . .

Psychologists call this a "tip-of-the-tongue state." You know a word, you use it regularly, but your brain refuses to access it. Studies show that people between the ages of eighteen and twenty-two experience this state about once or twice a week. Those between the ages of sixty-five and seventy-five lose words about twice as often. Sometimes a word pops into mind in a few seconds. Sometimes it takes days.

In the past, researchers speculated that the problem stemmed from a common word blocking a word that was similar to it. More recent studies suggest that people have the hardest time recalling a

W

word like "duplicate" which is less common and sounds like few other words. Apparently the brain needs a bigger push to ferret out words we use less frequently.

Finding a word is actually a two-stage process. First the brain accesses the concept, and then it searches for the sound of the word to match the meaning. Something similar happens when you see a familiar face but you can't recall the person's name. Distinct nerve cell circuits serve the part of the brain that stores the visual information and another processes the word—the person's name.

Often people remember the first letter of the word or name, or a similar sounding word comes to mind. According to Deborah M. Burke, a psychology professor at Pomona College in Claremont, California, people are twice as likely to find the word if they read or hear something that shares some of the missing word's sounds.

A Dutch researcher, Willem Levelt of the Max Planck Institute for Psycholinguistics, used advanced brain-imaging technology to solve the problem. He likens tip-of-the-tongue to a traffic jam of the brain. He says the harder you try to find the word, the harder it becomes. Most people have had the experience of remembering the word an hour after the relevant conversation ended. It just "pops up." So far, the experts do not know why. What they can tell you . . . Cucumber. That's the word I was looking for. Cucumber.

W

WORRY

Worry seems like preparation, but it is not. To prepare for something you have to do something. Most people prefer worry because it is much easier. You can do it sitting in your chair or in the shower or even lying in bed at night—especially lying in bed at night. It even feels kind of responsible, "See, I'm not ignoring the problem, I'm worrying about it."

Of course, worry is nothing new (in 1907 Caleb Williams Saleeby published a book with the title *Worry, the Disease of the Age*) and it will probably never go away. The same wonderful aspect of the brain that permits us to daydream and plan for the future also causes us to imagine worst-case scenarios. We are creative beings, which means that we are by nature problem-solving creatures. If we don't have a present problem to occupy our consciousness, a future one will do nicely.

In Shakespeare's day, when Hamlet spoke about "apprehension," he meant something else entirely. "What a piece of work is a man! How noble in reason! . . . in apprehension how like a god!" Back then, apprehension simply meant understanding. Now, four centuries later, it has taken on the tinge of anxiety. How did such a shift happen? I don't know, but I'm not going to worry about it too much.

When we envision bad things that have yet to happen, our "fight-or-flight" responses kick in. Since the things we fear have not yet happened, and may never happen, we can't really fight them so we try to flee them, but where do you go to flee your imagination? We end up frozen with nothing to do but worry more.

For example, creativity researcher Teresa Amabile of the Harvard Business School studied a 6,000-person division in a global electronics company during the course of a 25 percent downsizing. If you have ever worked for a company undergoing such a process, her findings will not surprise you. As people worried about their security, they disengaged from the work. Every measure of creativity in the work

W

environment went down significantly and it stayed down more than five months after the downsizing ended. Worrying about a potential job loss was more painful and draining for most than the job loss itself.

Worrying has little to do with your circumstances and everything to do with your proclivity to worry. Dr. Tony Bates, a clinical psychologist, told the *Irish Times* that some people prefer to worry about the future so they don't have to deal with the present. "We may also worry so as not to think about what's really bothering us," he said. "When our minds are dominated by worry, our memories and emotions become temporarily suppressed as the body prepares to deal with some imminent threat. Worrying about unlikely dangers may allow us to avoid thinking about the current issues that are undermining our sense of safety in the present."

By the way, a team of researchers at Concordia University in Montréal, Canada, examined people's perceptions of gender roles and worry and compared these perceptions to how worried men and women actually reported themselves to be. Participants believed women would be more worried about relationships and men would worry more about achievement and finances; they were wrong. In fact, they discovered that while women were slightly more prone to worry about relationships they also tended to report more worry about achievement than men did. Women, various studies seem to indicate, worry more than men in general.

British stress expert Roger Henderson recently published a study on what he calls "money sickness syndrome," which is debt stress that can be so severe it leads to skin rashes, shortness of breath, nausea, irritability, an inability to concentrate, and heart palpitations. One in five couples in the study had such severe money worry that it affected their love life. Again women were especially likely to report a loss of libido due to worry.

A Purdue University study from 2007 seems to confirm that worry can kill you. The twelve-year study of 1,663 men between the ages of forty-three and ninety-one revealed that the subjects who were the most neurotic, that is, inclined to worry over relatively minor

W

setbacks, were 40 percent more likely to die during the study. This does not bode well for Woody Allen.

Since worry was the "disease of the age" at the turn of the last century, let's see what they had to say about it at the time. Writing in 1919, George Lincoln Walton, author of *Why Worry?* (you didn't know they had self-help books back then, did you?) wrote: "I cannot expect to be wholly immune from the misfortunes of mankind . . . If we fret about the weather it is because of an insistent desire that the weather shall conform to our idea of its seasonableness . . . Suppose now, instead of devoting all our attention to the weather we should reason somewhat as follows: As long as I live on this particular planet, I shall be subject perhaps three days out of four, to atmospheric conditions which do not suit me. Is it worth my while to fret during those three days and to make it up by being elated on the fourth? . . . Or, as someone has said, why not 'make friends with the weather?' If one will cultivate this frame of mind he will be surprised to find that a certain physical relief will follow."

This gibes with what Dr. Ethel Quayle, lecturer at the University College Cork, had to say about worry: don't worry about it.

"The more we worry about the detrimental effects of worrying, the more of a problematic state it becomes," she told the *Irish Times*, ". . . The very process of trying to control private events, like thoughts, makes us hypersensitive to having them and is an increasing source of worry itself."

W

XMAS FOR CHRISTMAS

X

X = CHI

XMAS FOR CHRISTMAS

Merry Xmas. It's meant as a holiday greeting, but to many, the "X" is a big irritant. Some dislike it because it's inelegant and not the way people speak. Others find it aggravating for religious reasons.

"Since someone mentioned that using 'Xmas' is taking the 'Christ' out of Christmas, I have never written 'Xmas,'" wrote a *Calgary Sun* reader. "Maybe a weird little hang-up, but working in reverse, every time I see the word 'Xmas' it's a little reminder to me that Christ belongs in Christmas!"

It may seem that Xmas is a symbol of our modern, secularized, commercialized, "I wanna video drone" Christmas. (By the way, while we're on the subject of holiday irritants, it seems that a selfie stick with a microphone for portable karaoke was one of the hot gifts recently.) Xmas, however, dates back to the sixteenth century. The X is a stand in for the Greek letter *chi*, which resembles our X. The name of Christ in Greek was Xristos, thus chi represented Christ. Its shape was also reminiscent of the cross. For these two reasons, chi was used regularly in religious contexts. The ninth-century *Book of Kells* contains a lavishly decorated chi-rho page. In the sixteenth century, the use of Xmas spread throughout Europe along with such words as "Xren" for "christen" and "Xtian" for "Christian." Christians of that time would, therefore, immediately recognize the "Christ" in "Xmas." We no longer do. Xmas is easier to fit into headlines and advertisements, however, which contributes to the modern perception that it is an attempt to secularize the holiday.

As for that other winter holiday spelling problem—Hanukkah, Hanuka, Chanukah . . . which is it? The answer is, it depends. Hanukkah is translated from Hebrew, which has a different alphabet. When linguists translate from a language that has a different set of characters, they try to approximate the sound with the letters of the second language as best they can. Hanukkah literally means "dedication." It refers to the rededication of the Temple in Jerusalem after it had been defiled by the Syrians. The first letter of the word is the Hebrew *het*, which is pronounced like the "ch" in the Scottish word loch. German, and thus the German-influenced Yiddish, pronounce the "ch" similarly, unlike in English where we would tend to see "ch" and pronounce it as in "chalk." Originally, the name of the holiday was transcribed Chanukkah. Because English speakers tended to pronounce Chanukkah incorrectly, the spelling evolved to begin with "H", which is a better English approximation. We still don't pronounce it quite right, but at least we get closer than when we try to pronounce it with a "Ch."

As for the middle of the word and the one k or two question— Hebrew has two letters that correspond to our K, *kaf* and *kof*. Hanukkah uses kaf, which has a stronger "k" sound. For that reason, it is often translated as a double K, but there aren't many words with two ks in English, thus, the double K doesn't convey much meaning to us and it is often dropped. As for the "h" at the end, it doesn't change the sound of "ah" and it is sometimes dropped. The most frequent variations you will see are Hanukkah or Chanukah.

X

Y

YELLOW SPOTS ON PUBLIC TOILET SEATS, OR IF YOU SPRINKLE WHILE YOU TINKLE . . .

So you think men's restrooms are dirtier and grimier than women's? You're wrong. Dr. Charles Gerba, an Arizona microbiologist, has made a career of studying the places where germs lurk. As it turns out, women's facilities tend to have more harmful germs than men's. The researcher guesses this is because more children use them, putting the blame on young boys with bad aim.

There is another possibility. Women's restrooms have more bacteria because women use them. To avoid sitting on a dirty public toilet seat, many women squat or hover just above the bowl. It is not an easy task and they often miss the mark leaving drips and splashes on the seat.

The number of yellow drops has been increasing in stalls across America. It is a problem that builds upon itself. The more women feel they are unsanitary, the more likely they are to hover. According to one study (yes, of course people study this) about 59 percent of women now relieve themselves in this manner.

Let's dispel a few myths. You can't catch venereal disease from toilet seats. To put it as delicately as possible, the parts of the anatomy that would carry sexually transmitted diseases do not actually come into contact with the toilet seat.

As Gerba told a *Salon* reporter, "You don't catch things off your butt. You catch things off your hands."

In the course of his research, Gerba learned that only one out of fifty-nine public restroom toilet seats has E. coli bacteria on it. He found much more bacteria on the sinks. Another study three years later revealed that the kitchen is much germier than the average bathroom. There are more than 200 times more fecal bacteria on a

Y

cutting board (from raw meat) than on the home toilet seat. "If you have a choice between licking a toilet seat or a cutting board, go with the toilet seat," Gerba said.

The biggest danger from toilet seats is actually from injury, not disease. Between 2002 and 2010, there were 13,175 injuries related to the toilet or toilet seat. As with most categories of injury, the bulk of these are from slipping and cracking various body parts on them. There is another significant form of toilet injury, however, and it mostly involves young boys. Falling toilet seats injure about one hundred boys a year. The majority of these crush incidents are painful and embarrassing but not serious or long-lasting, but I digress.

A simple solution to the tinkle-sprinkle problem is for women to do what men do. No, I don't mean standing to pee. Boys learn, early on, to lift the toilet seat to avoid hosing it. If women do not want to sit on the seat, there is no reason why they should not lift it as well.

Y

59 percent of women do not sit on seat while urinating

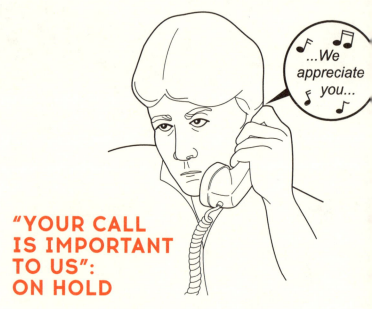

...We appreciate you...

"YOUR CALL IS IMPORTANT TO US": ON HOLD

My call is not important to you! If my call were so important to you, you'd answer it! An item from the "I could have told you that for free" file: a study conducted for Prudential Insurance of America found that 41 percent of Americans surveyed grew "angrier and angrier by the minute" when put on hold. What else drives us crazy? I'll give you a hint:

"Yes."
"Something Else."
"Agent."
"Agent!"

Yes, it is voice recognition technology. We hate shouting at robots so much that most people only call customer service after they've exhausted all other avenues. The first place most people go to get

Y

answers is the company's web page. By the time you've given in and picked up the phone, it is unlikely that your question is common enough to be part of a phone tree and having to wade through a menu of options that don't fit is one of life's little frustrations.

The silver lining is that companies are trying to use the dreaded technology to reduce your irritation. It doesn't help them to have disgruntled customers. One way they entertain you while on hold, surprisingly enough, is to bombard you with commercials. We complain about them, but in spite of what we say, messages on hold keep us on the line. A Nationwide Insurance study shows that on-hold messaging reduces hang-ups by 50 to 80 percent. In fact, 15 to 35 percent of callers responded to the advertising messages and bought additional items.

They have also been experimenting with hold music. Karen Niven, a lecturer at Manchester Business School in England, studied the effects of different types of music on customer's moods. The results were published in the *Journal of Applied Social Psychology* in 2014. Niven guessed that popular music with pro-social lyrics, like Michael Jackson's "Heal the World" would make people most cooperative and happy. She tested the hypothesis by changing the music at a call center to play either standard pop music, pro-social pop music, or a control of instrumental music. The results surprised Niven. The callers who listened to pop music were less angry than those who had heard the instrumental "elevator music," but they were equally annoyed by the pro-social music. It seems the contrast between healing the world and being placed on hold got their dander up. If pop music makes us happy why don't more companies use it? Licensing fees.

The good news is that voice-recognition systems are getting smarter, and most are programmed to detect anger and frustration. In a lot of systems, you will be transferred to a human being if you shout a few choice words into the receiver.

Thank you for continuing to hold. Your call is important to us. Please hold for a message from our sponsor . . .

Y

ZIPPERS

Z

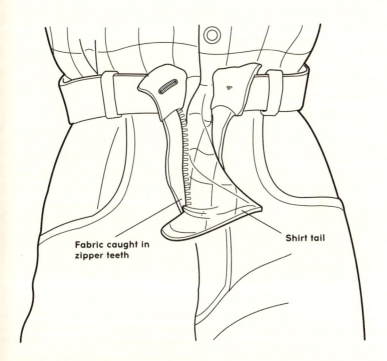

Fabric caught in zipper teeth

Shirt tail

ZIPPERS, STUCK

The metal-toothed clothing fastener dates back to 1891 and a Chicago inventor named Whitcomb Judson. It wasn't until 1917 that a Swedish engineer named Gideon Sunback updated the design so it resembled the fastener we know today. The word "zipper" began life as a trade name. The BFGoodrich company marketed a model of galoshes with a hookless fastener. The brand name of the shoes was soon applied to their new-fangled fastener. As zippers gained popularity, more were able to experience the joys of having a zip stick at an inopportune moment.

If you take a close look at a zipper—to avoid misunderstandings you should probably make it your own—you will see that it is made up of a slider with a pull that runs over two rows of molded metal or plastic teeth which are shaped in such a way that they interlock. Most

Z

often it is the slider that breaks down. If you find your zipper just won't zip, or if it has the unfortunate habit of leaving you exposed to the public, the slider is probably worn or bent out of shape. Ditto if it seems welded in place. A common way for sliders to become bent is fabric that gets caught in the zip's teeth. Pull the thread out of the zip. If you still can't get the thing open, you can try greasing the zipper with crayons, candles, soap, or lip balm. Once you get the offending item off, you can fix the slider by gently squeezing it back into shape with a pair of pliers. "Gently" is the active word here. You want to squeeze it just enough to keep it from sliding down the teeth or open it just enough to move freely, not enough to seal it shut or break it in half. If the zipper is missing teeth or it is coming off the fabric all together, this is more complicated. If you can sew, you can fix it. If you can't, call a tailor.

While we're on the subject of stuck zippers, briefly, here's what *Men's Health* has to say about getting stuck in your zipper. While it is extremely rare that anyone gets his entire member stuck like the boy in the movie *There's Something About Mary*, minor mishaps do happen. Zipper accidents usually result in superficial skin injuries but they are still painful enough to make number three on the magazine's list of the "8 Worst Things You Can Do to Your Privates." Contrary to popular belief, most zipper injuries occur when unzipping, not zipping. If you find yourself in this position, *Men's Health* advises you pull the zipper in the direction it came from in one swift motion. Then assess the damage and, if necessary, apply a bandage to stop the bleeding.

Z

BIBLIOGRAPHY

AAA Foundation for Traffic Safety. Aggressive Driving Research Update, April, 2009. Accessed January 4, 2017. https://www.aaafoundation.org/sites/default/files/AggressiveDrivingResearchUpdate2009.pdf.

Adams, Cecil. "Everything You Ever Wanted to Know About Farts." The Straight Dope [syndicated column], Chicago Reader, Inc., 1996.

———. "Why is the Sound of Fingernails Scraping a Blackboard so Annoying?" The Straight Dope [syndicated column], Chicago Reader, Inc., 1996.

Aisling, Irwin. "Scientists Get the Art of Dunking Down to a T." The Daily Telegraph, November 25, 1998.

Ajluni, Cheryl. "Static elimination technology rids computer screens and television sets of static electric fields." Electronic Design, November 18, 1996.

All Things Considered (NPR). "Scientists Look for Commonalities in Annoying Sounds." May 12, 1996.

Allison, Wes. "The Worst Job Ever? Paid Patients Unzip to Aid Med Students." The Washington Times, January 15, 2001.

Allmon, Stephanie. "The Privy Truth: Toilet Seats Getting a Bad Rap." Palm Beach Post, May 16, 2000.

Andersen, Erika. "Courageous Leaders Don't Make Excuses. They Apologize." Forbes. June 5, 2012.

Andrews, Linda Wassmer, "How to Stress Less in a Traffic Jam." Psychology Today, September 2, 2015.

Asbell, Bernard and Karen Wynn. What They Know About You. New York: Random House, 1991.

Ashford, Molika, "Evidence that Traffic Tickets Aren't Just About Road Safety." Scientific American, January 21, 2009.

Associated Press. "Why won't that machine take my dollar?" Arlington Morning News, May 30, 1999.

Barnett, Brian, "Want Safer Passwords? Don't Change Them So Often." Wired, March 10, 2016.

———. "You Can Finally Delete the Junk Apps on Your Phone." Wired, June 13, 2016.

Bayley, Ed, "The Clicks That Bind, Ways Users Agree to Online Contracts." Electronic Frontier Foundation, November 16, 2009.

BBC News Online Network. "No More Flunking on Dunking." November 25, 1998.

Bernstein, Joseph, "Too Many Passwords to Remember." Buzzfeed, May 4, 2016.

Blair, James W. "Cost-Cutting Cops Seek to Avoid False Alarms." *The Christian Science Monitor*, February 24, 1998.

Bloomer, Jeffrey. "Political Posts." *Slate*. March 12, 2012.

Bordsen, John, "Science Briefs: Always Checking Your Device? It's Impulse." (Charlotte) *News & Observer*, March 20, 2016.

Bowen, Jon. "Personal-space Invaders." *Salon*, September 1, 1999.

Bowles, Scott. "Aggressive ticketing has drivers feeling trapped." *USA Today*, September 3, 1999.

Brehm, Alison S. and Cathy Lee, "From the Chair, Click Here to Accept Terms of Service." *Communications Lawyer*, January 2015.

Brodeur, Raymond, D. C., PhD. "The audible release associated with joint manipulation." *Journal of Manipulative and Physiological Therapeutics* 18, no.3 (March/April 1995): 155–64.

Brody, Jane. "Slaying a Case of Dragon Mouth." *Minneapolis Star Tribune*, March 23, 1997.

———. "Solid Old: Radio Dials for Dollars by Programming More and More of the Past." *The Dallas Morning News*, November 14, 1998.

Bryant, Furlow. "The Smell of Love: How Women Rate the Sexiness and Pleasantness of a Man's Body." *Psychology Today*, March 13, 1996.

Burkeman, Oliver. "Keep Your Distance." *The Guardian* [UK], September 14, 1999.

Butler, David. "Best Alarm is Not False." *Minneapolis Star Tribune*, March 21, 1996

Butler, Jerry. "Mosquitoes Have Discriminating Tastes, UF Researchers Find." Press Release. August 20, 1999.

Capitol Hill Press Release. "Murkowski Praises UAL Decision to Add Space Between Airline Seats." August 6, 1999.

Carey, Stan. "Sorry Not Sorry." *Slate*, November 20, 2014.

Carlson, Peter. "Playing the Waiting Game; Stuck in Line at the ATM? Still On Hold for the Doctor? Got Something Better to Do With Your Time? Here, Read This." *The Washington Post*, December 14, 1999.

Carter, Andrew. "15 Things More Likely to Happen Than Winning Mega Millions." *The Daily Beast*, March 30, 2012.

Cartwright, Jon. "The Physics of Spilled Coffee." *Science*, May 4, 2012.

Castellanos, Jorge and David Axelrod, "Effect of Habitual Knuckle Cracking on Hand Function." *Annals of Rheumatic Diseases* 49 (1990): 308–9.

Catlett, Jason. "What Can Be Done About Junk E-Mail?" *USA Today Magazine*, November 1, 1998.

Chebat, Jean-Charles-Gelinas et al. "The Impact of Mood on Time Perceptions, Memorization and Acceptance of Waiting." *Genetic, Social and General Psychology Monographs*, November 1, 1995: 413–24.

Christensen, Damaris. "Is Snoring a DiZZZZease?" *Science News*, March 11, 2000.

Chism, Olin. "Show must go on, but coughs must go off." *The Dallas Morning News*, August 25, 1996.

Christman, Laura. "In Your Dust: We're Talking About the Common Household Variety—It's a Veritable Breakdown of Your Life." *Newsday*, March 26, 1998.

Connor, Steve. "Biscuit Dunking Perfected." *The Independent*, November 25, 1998.

Considine, Austin. "Defriended, Not De-Emoted." *The New York Times*, September 3, 2010.

Coren, Stanley. "Why Do Dogs Like to Sniff Crotches?" *Psychology Today*, August 7, 2014.

Corey, Mary. "Raising a Stink over Scent." *The Evening Post* (Wellington, New Zealand), September 20, 1995.

Coventry, John et al. "Periodontal disease. (ABC of Oral Health)." *British Medical Journal* 321, no. 7252 (July 1, 2000): 36–39.

Cox, Kate. "New Online Tool Tells You What the Heck Privacy Policies Actually Say." *Consumerist*, March 11, 2016.

Cranor, Lorrie. "Time to Rethink Mandatory Password Changes." Federal Trade Commission. March 2, 2016. https://www.ftc.gov/news-events/blogs/techftc/2016/03/time-rethink-mandatory-password-changes.

Decker, Denise. "A Woman's Guide to How to Pee Standing Up." www.theplacewithnoname.com/t/Peestanding.pdf.

Dermatology Times. "Hangnails." July 2000.

Desrocher, Jack. "Oral ecology." *Technology Review*, January 1, 1997.

Digital Learning Center for Microbial Ecology. "Habitat on Humanity." Michigan State University Communication Technology Laboratory Center for Microbial Ecology, 2000.

DiPacio, Bonnie. "Why are Clowns So Scary to Some? Figures of Fantasy both Attract, Repel." *The Dallas Morning News*, January 17, 1999.

Disalvo, David. "How to Tell if Someone is Lying." *Psychology Today*, March 16, 2012.

Discover. "Snooze Alarm: Snoring and Your Health." July 1, 1999.

Drake, Petra. Email correspondence with author. April, 2001.

Duenwald, Mary, "Need Reading Glasses? Welcome to Middle Age." *The New York Times*, June 8, 2004.

Dufner, Edward. "Experts Call Virus Writers High-Tech, Low-Brow." *The Dallas Morning News*, April 1, 1999.

Eagan, James M. *A Speeder's Guide to Avoiding Tickets.* New York: Avon Books, 1990.

Ebeling, Walter. "Urban Entomology." University of California, Division of Agricultural Sciences, 1996.

The Economist. "Stickiness: Blame it on the Bubbles." January 23, 1999.

eHow. "How to Fix a Dry Ballpoint Pen." Accessed April 25, 2012. www.ehow.com/how_2383970_ fix_dry_ballpoint-pen.html.

Ehrlich, Robert. *Why Toast Lands Jelly-Side Down.* Princeton, New Jersey: Princeton University Press, 1997.

Engbear, Daniel. "Who Made That Pop-Up Ad." *The New York Times Magazine*, February 14, 2014.

Ettus, Samantha, ed. *The Experts' Guide to Life at Home.* New York: Clarkson Potter, 2005.

Evans, Sandra. "Send In the Clowns, But Not Too Close." *The Washington Post*, March 28, 2000.

Everbach, Tracy. "Huh? Academic Jargon is the Language of a Closed Club Among Scholars." *The Dallas Morning News*, July 6, 1999.

Feltman, Rachel and Sarah Kaplan. "Dear Science. How Do I Stop Snoring?" *The Washington Post*, August 22, 2016.

Finberg, Kathy. "Telemarketing Calls are Not Good RX." *The Arizona Republic*, March 9, 1999.

Fisher, Anne. "Best Business Books: Excuse Me, Please, Do You Mind If I Sell You Something?" *Fortune*, June 21, 1999.

Fishman, Charles. "But Wait, You Promised . . ." *Fast Company*, April 1, 2001.

Flatow, Ira. "Analysis: How the Sense of Smell Operates." Talk of the Nation Science Friday (NPR), March 10, 2000.

———. "Analysis: Types and habits of some of the many insects that reappear as spring comes." Talk of the Nation Science Friday (NPR), March 24, 2000.

Food Institute Report. "Carry On Meals And Fly." January 26, 1999.

Forsman, Theresa. "To Zagat Reviewers, Good Service Sells." The Record (Bergen County, N.J.), September 2, 1999.

Fumento, Michael. "Senseless Scent Patrol." The Washington Times, May 7, 2000.

Gapper, John. "Resolve to Kick the Addiction to Work Emails." The Financial Times, January 4, 2017.

Gardiner, Martin. "On Being Annoyed." Improbable Research (blog), August 12, 2015. http://www.improbable.com/2015/08/12/on-being-annoyed/.

Gardiner, Martin. "Towards Quantifying Snoring Annoyance." Improbable Research, (blog), April 13, 2010. http://www.improbable.com/2010/04/13/towards-quantifying-snoring-annoyance/

Getchell, Annie. "Zipper Mending: How to Make Quick-Fixes and Permanent Repairs." Backpacker, August 1, 1996.

Gilbert, Ben. "It's Not Just You: Terms of Service Agreements Really Are Confusing, Study Finds." Endgadget, April 17, 2014.

Glanz, James. "No Hope of Silencing the Phantom Crinklers of the Opera." The New York Times, June 1, 2000.

Glausiusz, Josie. "The Root of All Itching." Discover, April 2001.

Goddard, Peter. "The Science Behind the Scent." The Toronto Star, January 11, 2001.

Goldman, Jason G. "The Curious Truth About Belly Button Fluff." BBC, July 10, 2015.

Goldman, Michael. "Clowns are No Laughing Matter." The Toronto Star, July 8, 2000.

Gorman, Christine. "Shake, Rattle and Roar. Thunder in the Distance? No, It's a Boom Car Coming." Time, March 6, 1989.

Gott, Peter. "Tomato Juice and the Piles." The Ottawa Sun, June 17, 2000.

Graedon, Joe and Theresa Graedon. "The People's Pharmacy: How to be Unattractive to the Mosquitoes." Newsday, August 14, 2000.

Gray, Richard. "Do You Suffer From Password Rage?" The Daily Mail, June 8, 2015.

———. "Get That Song Out of Your Head." The Telegraph, March 24, 2013.

———. "The Science of Brain Freeze." The Daily Mail, May 4, 2015.

Griest, Stephanie. "Telemarketers Often Get Wrung Out by the Stress in their Work." *Minneapolis Star Tribune*, July 14, 1995.

Griffiths, Mark D. "All Trolled Up." *Psychology Today*, March 17, 2014.

Groves, Bob. "Calming the ZZZZZZs." *The Record* (Bergen County, N.J.), January 18, 1993.

Gubbins, Teresa. "What About MY Space?" *The Dallas Morning News*, February 23, 2000.

Guo, Jeff. "How Your Junk Mail Shows if You're Rich or Poor." *The Washington Post*, October 19, 2015.

———. "Men, Women and Ikea, It's Complicated." *The Washington Post*, December 17, 2015.

Haege, Glenn. "Stop Mosquitoes from Bugging You with Several Simple Solutions." Gannett News Service, August 22, 2000.

Hai, Dorothy M. "Sex and the Single Armrest: Use of Personal Space During Air Travel." *Psychological Reports* 51, no. 3 (1982): 743–49.

Hansen, Laura. "Dialing for Dollars." *Marketing Tools*, January/February 1997.

Harley, Trevor A., and Helen E. Brown. "What causes a tip-of-the-tongue state? Evidence for lexical neighbourhood effects in speech production." *British Journal of Psychology* 89, no. 1 (February 1998): 151–74.

Harrison, Virginia and Jose Paglieri. "Nearly 1 Million New Malware Threats Released Every Day." CNN, April 14, 2015.

Haubrich, William S. *Medical Meanings: A Glossary of Word Origins.* Philadelphia: American College of Physicians, 1997.

Hawkins, Katherine. Telephone interview by author, March 13, 2001.

Hayden, Thomas. "The Scent of Human." *U.S. News & World Report*, March 26, 2001.

Hecht, Julie. "The Real Reasons Dogs Sniff Crotches." *Business Insider*, January 5, 2013.

Hellmich, Nanci. "Sharing Tips for Both Waiters and Diners." *USA Today*, June 22, 1994.

Herman, John. "Why the Progress Bar Is Lying to You." *Popular Mechanics*, February 27, 2012.

Hill, Kashmir. "How to Keep Trolls and Harassers from Winning." *Forbes*, August 21, 2014.

Horn, Leslie. "Infographic: Why Do People Unfriend Each Other on Facebook?" *PC Magazine Online*, December 19, 2011.

Huffington Post. "Free Time is More Important than Money: Study." January 12, 2016.

Hulihan, J. "Ice cream headache." *British Medical Journal* 314 (1997).

Huntington, Sharon. "On the Trail of Dust." *The Christian Science Monitor*, August 17, 1999.

Huston, Aletha C. et al. *Big World, Small Screen: The Role of Television in American Society.* Lincoln, Nebraska: University of Nebraska Press, 1992.

Hutchins, Chris. "Brain Freeze! Is There No Escape From That Icy Ache?" *Arlington Morning News*, July 18, 1999.

Hyde, Justin. "Detroit to Push Cars that Warn of Traffic Jams." *The Toronto Star*, October 23, 2000.

———. "Ice Cream Headaches, Nerves Tied." *The Arizona Republic*, February 15, 2000.

———. "If the Movie Trailer's Rockin' Don't Bother Knockin' It." *The Toronto Star*, January 20, 1999.

Incantalupo, Tom. "Alarming. Even Turning Your Car into an Electronic Fortress May Not Keep it Safe." *St. Louis Post-Dispatch*, October, 30, 1993.

Ingram, Jay. "Why Candy Wrappers Can Wreck Your Night Out." *The Toronto Star*, July 16, 2000.

Irvine, Pru. "@/+!='!****!!! Road Rage Has Got Nothing on This." *The Independent*, December 11, 1997.

Jacobson, Louis. "Sensor-Based Cruise Control Keeps Cars Apart." *The Washington Post*, September 4, 2000.

Jacobsson, Sarah. "Surprise: Facebook Friends Aren't Real Friends." *PC World*, January 25, 2010.

James, Leon and Diane Nahl. Telephone interview by author. January 24, 2001.

———. *Road Rage and Aggressive Driving: Steering Clear of Highway Warfare.* Amherst, NY: Prometheus Books, 2000.

Jaret, Peter. "What Pests Want in Your Home." *National Wildlife*, August 1, 1999.

Jarrett, Christian. "This Mental Quirk Could Explain Why You're Always Running Late." *BPS Research Digest*, October 27, 2016.

Jenkins, Milly. "A Virus is Not Always the Product of a Sick Mind." *The Independent*, January 13, 1998.

Kadir, Rahimah A. "Plaque—The Hidden Enemy." *New Straits Times*, February 1, 1998.

Kanner, Bernice. *Are You Normal?* New York: St. Martin's, 1995.

Karger, Dave. "Trailer Trash: Are Movie Previews Giving Away Too Much These Days?" *Entertainment Weekly*, July 10, 1998.

Karp, Hal. "Car Seat Safety Check: 8 Common Mistakes You Must Avoid." *Parents*, January 1, 2003.

Katayama, Lisa. *Urawaza: Secret Everday Tips and Tricks from Japan*. San Francisco: Chronicle Books, 2008.

Kelleher, Kathleen. "The Word is . . . I know, It's Right on the Tip of My Tongue." *Minneapolis Star Tribune*, April 9, 1997.

Kelly, Sara, "When Bad Breath Happens to Good People." *Men's Health*, October 1, 1996.

Klein, Richard. "Get a Whiff of This: Breaking the Smell Barrier." *The New Republic*, February 6, 1995.

Koepp, Stephen. "Gridlock: Congestion on Americas Highways and Runways Takes a Grinding Toll." *Time*, September 12, 1998.

KSEE News. "Car Seats Breed Confusion," Accessed May 19, 2012. https://web.archive.org/web/20120415152922/http://www.ksee24.com/news/local/Study-Child-Seats-Breed-Frustration-147265235.html.

LaFrance, Adrienne. "The First Pop-Up Ad." *The Atlantic*, August 14, 2014.

Larson, Jan. "Surviving Commuting." *American Demographics*, July, 1998.

Lee, Laura. *Don't Screw It Up*. White Plains, NY: Reader's Digest, 2013.

Lehndorff, John. "A Tip to the Wise. Poor Service Has Driven Some Diners to Get Tough." *Denver Rocky Mountain News*, October 19, 2000.

Lilienfeld, Scott O. et al. *50 Great Myths of Popular Psychology: Shattering Widespread Misconceptions about Human Behavior*. London: Wiley-Blackwell, 2009.

Lipscomb, Betsy. Telephone Interview by Author. April 4, 2001.

Loder, Amanda. "How Junk Mail Is Helping to Prop Up the Postal Service." *State Impact*, September 27, 2011.

Lupien, Sonia. Telephone Interview by Author. March 22, 2001.

MacDonald, Fiona. "There's a Surprisingly Awesome Reason for the Holes on Top of Pen Caps." *Science Alert*, May 2, 2016.

Madrigal, Alexis. "Reading the Privacy Policies You Encounter in a Year Would Take 76 Work Days." *The Atlantic*, March 1, 2012.

Maleshefski, Tiffany. "How Does Plastic Wrap Cling?" *Chowhound*, April 17, 2008.

Manjoo, Farhad. "Web Trolls Winning as Incivility Increases." *The New York Times*, August 14, 2014.

Manjoo, Farahad. "Why Streaming Movie Services Fail to Satisfy." *The New York Times*, March 26, 2014.

Martin, Hugo. "White House Report Slams Hidden Fees Charged by Hotels, Airlines, Other Businesses." *The Los Angeles Times*, January 7, 2017.

Masnick, Mike. "To Read All of the Privacy Policies You Encounter You'd Need to Take a Week Off Work Every Year." *Tech Dirt*, April 23, 2012.

Masoff, Joy. *Oh Yuck! The Encyclopedia of Everything Nasty.* New York: Workman Publishing, 2000.

Matthews, Robert. "Odd Socks: A Cominatoric Example of Murphy's Law." *Mathematics Today*, March–April 1996.

———. "Tumbling toast, Murphy's Law and the fundamental constants." *European Journal of Physics* 16 (1995): 172–73.

———. "Why Some Words Just Will Not Trip Off the Tongue." *The Sunday Telegraph.* May 31, 1998.

Mayer, Caroline. "Today's Specials: Waiters with Professional Training." *St. Louis Post-Dispatch*, April 13, 1993.

Mayo Clinic. "Car Seat Safety: Avoid 10 Common Mistakes." Accessed May 19, 2012. http://www.mayoclinic.com/health/car-seat-safety/MY00824.

McAndrew, Francis T. Telephone interview by author, March 28, 2001.

McCartney, Scott. "Fee Squished? Airlines Are Shrinking Headroom, Too." *The Wall Street Journal*, December 8, 2016.

McCluggage, Denise. "For Safe Driving, Have a Clear Outlook." *The Washington Times*, July 2, 1999.

McCunn, Lindsey. "Sound or Noise?" *Psychology Today*, November 20, 2014.

McGee, Bill. "Think Airline Seats Have Gotten Smaller? They Have." *USA Today*, September 24, 2014.

McGregor, Jay. "Man Who Invented Pop-Up Ads Says I'm Sorry." *Forbes*, August 15, 2014.

McKay, Martha. "Nuisance Calls Hit New Highs." *The Record* (Bergen County, N.J.), January 30, 2000.

McMillan, Robert. "Turns Out Your Complex Passwords Aren't That Much Safer." *Wired*, August 11, 2014.

McNamee, Laurence and Kent Biffle. "Funny Bone?" *The Dallas Morning News*, January 12, 1997.

McRaney, David. *You Are Not So Smart.* New York: Penguin, 2011.

Medical Update. "My Doctor Said I Don't Need Surgery for My Hemorrhoids!" August 1, 1994.

Medical Post. "It's Enough to Make You Sick [Word Origins]." November 17, 1999.

Mejia, Brittny. "Unfriending Could Have Psychological Impact." *Arizona Wildcat*. January 11, 2012.

Mielach, David. "Facebook Unfriending Has Real Life Consequences." *Business News Daily*, February 5, 2013.

Mikkelson, David. "Facebook Privacy Notice." Snopes, October 14, 2016.

Milliken, Greg. "The Paperless Office: A Thirty Year Old Pipe Dream?" *Wired*. Accessed December 22, 2016. https://www.wired.com/insights/2014/01/paperless-office-30-year-old-pipe-dream/.

Mindess, Mary. Telephone interview by author. February 21, 2001.

Minneapolis Star Tribune. "Tricks of the Trailers: Draw 'Em In, But Spoil the Movie." October 26, 1999.

Mizejewski, Gerald. "Man gets breathing room after 10 years of hiccups." *The Washington Times*, March 25, 2000.

Mooney, Chris. "The Science of Why Comment Trolls Suck." *Mother Jones*, January 10, 2013.

Morran, Chris. "Senate Report Rips Airlines for Failing to Clearly Disclose Fees." *The Consumerist*, August 6, 2015.

Morris, Hugh, "Airsickness Bags: A Short History." *The Telegraph*, August 20, 2015.

Morris, Kaye. "How to Unclog Ballpoint Pens." eHow. www.ehow.com/how_6372064_unclog-ballpoint-pens.html.

Moscaritolo, Angela. "What Stresses Everyone Out, Buffering Videos, Apparently." *PC Magazine*, February 17, 2016.

Most, Doug. "Driving 65 MPH Is Good for Egos, *But Little Else.*" *The Record* (Bergen County, N.J.), February 2, 1998.

Munson, Marty. "Head Off Itches. (Controlling the Urge to Scratch)." *Prevention*, May 1, 1996.

Murphy, William. "It's Simply Alarming: Bill Would Ban Noisy Anti-Theft Devices on Cars." *Newsday*, April 28, 1997.

Myslinski, Norbert R. "Now Where Did I Put Those Keys?" *The World & I*, November 1, 1998.

NBC 4 New York. "These Are the Nine Biggest Earworm Songs." November 3, 2016. http://www.nbcnewyork.com/news/local/These-Are-the-9-Biggest-Earworm-Songs-399841491.html.

Newsday. "Take My Dandruff. . . . Please." December 12, 1994.

Nixon, Ron. "Seeking Revenue, Postal Service Plans to Deliver More Junk Mail." *The New York Times*, September 19, 2012.

Novotney, Amy. "Silence Please." *Monitor in Psychology*, JulyAugust, 2011.

Nunez, Daniel G. "Cause and Effects of Noise Pollution." Student Paper Interdisciplinary Minor in Global Sustainability, University of California, Irvine. Spring 1998. http://darwin.bio.uci.edu/sustain/global/sensem/S98/Nunez/Noise.html.

Obar, Jonathan and Anne Oledorf-Hirsch. "The Biggest Lie on the Internet: Ignoring the Privacy Policies and Terms of Service Policies of Social Networking Services." August 24, 2016. Available at SSRN: https://ssrn.com/abstract=2757465.

Okie, Susan. "Survivors: 350 Million Years Later, Cockroaches Are Still Going Strong." *The Washington Post*, November 10, 1999.

Olen, Helain. "Congratulations! You Lost!" *Slate*, May 24, 2016.

Pash, Adam. "Skip Straight to the Operator with Your Dirty Mouth." *Lifehacker*, June 8, 2006.

Patterson, Thom. "Airline Squeeze: It's Not You, It's the Seat." CNN, June 1, 2012.

Paul, Ian. "Goodbye Firstborn Children." *PC World*, July 13, 2016.

Paulus, Rick. "The Hidden Psychology of Wearing Glasses." *Pacific Standard*, January 27, 2015.

Perl, Peter. "Waking With the Enemy: He Never Quite Believed He Had a Snoring Problem Till He Slept Beside a Tape Recorder." *The Washington Post*, November 28, 1999.

Piesing, Mark. "The Web's Oldest Dark Art: Can Spam Be Canned?" *The Independent*, March 27, 2013.

Pilkington, Diana. "Looking for a Way to Rid Your Need of Reading Glasses?" *The Daily Mail*, March 21, 2016.

Plesance, Chris. "Is This the End of Spam E-mails?" *The Daily Mail*, July 18, 2015.

Post, Peggy, Lizzie Post, Anna Post, Daniel Post Senning. *Emily Post's Etiquette.* New York: Harper Collins, 2015. Kindle Edition.

Potkewitz, Hilary. "Can Your Relationship Handle a Trip to IKEA?" *The Wall Street Journal*, April 22, 2015.

Precker, Michael. "Germ Warfare from a Man Who's 'Written a Lot of Toilet Papers,'" *The Dallas Morning News*, July 20, 1998.

Psychology Today. "The Nose Knows." May, 2000.

Purthill, Corrine. "Why Ikea Causes So Much Relationship Tension." *The Atlantic*, September 20, 2015.

Quirk, Mary Beth. "Survey Confirms What Your Nose Already Knows." *The Consumerist*, January 29, 2014.

Randovsky, Louise. "White House Tallies Hours Spent Filling Out Forms." *The Wall Street Journal*, September 17, 2011.

Raphael, Michael. "This Space is Mine! Drivers Show Classic Apelike Behavior." Associated Press, May 13, 1997.

Reinstein, Julia. "Three Un-Fun Facts About the Psychology of Traffic to Read While You're Stuck in It." *New York Magazine*, May 23, 2014.

Rense, Sarah. "The Case for Ignoring Work Emails." *Esquire*, January 3, 2017.

Reynolds, Christopher. "Odds of Major U.S. Airlines Losing Your Baggage Are About One in 197." *Minneapolis Star Tribune*, July 16, 2000.

Rheingold, Howard. *They Have a Word For It*. Los Angeles: Jeremy P. Tarcher, Inc. 1988.

Richert, Mary. "My Remote, Myself." *The Guardian*, October 6, 2008.

Rivenburg, Roy. "Sound of Silence: It's Disquieting Are We Addicted to Noise?" *St. Louis Post-Dispatch*, July 28, 1997.

Roach, Mary. "Ladies Who Spray." *Salon*, May 19, 2000.

Robinson, John P., and Geoffrey Godbey. "The Great American Slowdown." *American Demographics*, June 1, 1996.

———. *Time for Life: The Surprising Ways Americans Use Their Time*. University Park, Pennsylvania: Pennsylvania State University Press, 1997.

Robinson, William. "What's the Top Pest?: Ants Are the Answer." *Pest Control*, April 1, 1999.

Rodinova, Zlata. "French Workers Win Right to Disconnect." *The Independent*, December 31, 2016.

Rosato, Donna. "Why Checking Email After Work Is Bad for Your Career and Health." *Fortune*, April 7, 2015.

Rose, Heidi. "Human Weakness Causes Virus Spread." *Computer Weekly*, August 3, 2000.

Rosenbaum, Thane. *The Myth of Moral Justice*. New York: Harper Collins, 2004.

Rosenbloom, Stephanie. "Fighting the Incredible Shrinking Airline Seat." *The New York Times*, February 29, 2016.

Rucki, Alexandra. "Average Smartphone User Checks Device 221 Times a Day, According to Research." *The Evening Standard*, October 7, 2014.

Ryan, Tim. "It Takes Americans 6.1 Billion Hours to Prepare Their Taxes says Virginia Foxx," Politifact, April 15, 2014.

Saketkhoo K, Januszkievicz A, Sackner MA. "Effects of drinking hot water, cold water, and chicken soup on nasal mucus velocity and nasal airflow resistance." *Chest* 74, no. 4 (1978): 408-10.

Sant, Charles. Email correspondence with author. November, 1997.

Sapsted, David. "Loud Music is As Addictive as Drugs and Alcohol." *The Daily Telegraph*, December 10, 1998.

Schwade, Steve. "Read This Before You Fly: Prevention's Flight Plan for Comfort and Health." *Prevention*, June 1, 1996.

Schwarcz, Joe. "Everyday Chemistry: What Makes a Situation Sticky." *The Washington Post*, December 8, 1999.

Schwartz, John. "No Love for Computer Bugs: A New Generation of Virus Hunters Learn the Craft." *The Washington Post*, July 5, 2000.

Science News. "Which is More Annoying, Spam or Direct Mail?" November 3, 2006.

Scott, John. "Road Rage." Fox Files (Fox News Network), June 22, 1999.

Sellgrren, Katherine. "Teenagers Checking Mobile Phones in the Night." *BBC News*, October 6, 2016.

Sewell, Diane. "6 Ways to Spot a Liar." *Reader's Digest Canada*. Accessed June 5, 2012. http://www.readers digest.ca/health/healthy-living/ 6-ways-spot-liar.

Shea, Christopher. "The Hidden Fee Economy." *The New York Times Magazine*, December 10, 2006.

Shultz, Colin. "The Story of Laszlo Biro, The Man Who Invented the Ballpoint Pen." *Smithsonian*, August 22, 2012.

Siegel, Robert. "Interview: Professor Eric Kramer, Simon's Rock College, Discusses the Scientific Reason Why Plastic Candy Wrappers Make Noise When You Unwrap Them." All Things Considered (NPR), June 1, 2000.

Simon, Scott. "Brain Freeze." Weekend Saturday (NPR), July 12, 1997.

Sisson, Patrick. "How Driverless Cars Can Reshape Our Cities." *Curbed*, February 25, 2016.

Sleigh, J. W. "Ice cream headache." *British Medical Journal* 315 (1997).

Smith, Dinitia. "When Ideas Get Lost in Bad Writing." *The New York Times*, February 27, 1999.

Smith, Ian K. "Personal Time: Your Health: Dangerous Seats? Crammed into Airline Economy Class You May Be Risking Blood Clots." *Time*, November 6, 2000.

Snead, Elizabeth. "Sneak Peeks. First Impressions Are the Most Important. Just Ask Anyone Who Saw the Trailer for The Postman." *USA Today*, May 1, 1998.

Snyder, Jodie. "It May Seem Funny, But No One Knows Why We Hic." *Minneapolis Star Tribune*, July 2, 1995.

Spilner, Maggie. "De-stress Your Commute." *Prevention*, March 1, 1995.

Stewart, Martha. "Hankies and Dust: Nothing to Sneeze At." *Newsday*, April 12, 2000.

Stockburger, Jennifer. "Common Mistakes When Installing Child Car Seats." *Consumer Reports*, September 17, 2010.

Stovsky, Renee. "No! No! Not Again. What Happens When Kids Love to Hear Books Their Parents Hate to Read?" *St. Louis Post-Dispatch*, September 5, 1993.

Subotky, Julie. *Consider It Done: Accomplish 228 of Life's Trickiest Tasks.* New York: Random House, 2001.

Sugarman, Carole. "Use it or Lose It; Do You Know When It's Time to Chuck the Chicken or Dump the Milk?" *The Washington Post*, October 11, 2000.

The Sun. "Ear We Go Again." August 6, 2016.

Suplee, Curt. "Get Outta My Space! The Science and Secrets of Personal Space." *The Washington Post*, June 9, 1999.

Sykes, Charles J. *A Nation of Victims.* New York: St. Martin's Press, 1992.

Tenner, Edward. *When Things Bite Back: Technology and the Revenge of Unintended Consequences.* New York: Alfred A. Knopf, 1996.

Tevlin, Jon. "Mechanically Declined; Going Nuts Trying to Put Together Simple Ikea Furnishings?" *Minneapolis Star Tribune*, June 22, 2005.

Thomas, Rhys, H. and Naomi J. P. Thomas. "Miracle hiccough cure gets the attention it deserves." *British Medical Journal* 333, no. 7580 (2006): 2222.

Uhlig, Robert. "Bad Breath Detector Has the Measure of Halitosis." *The Daily Telegraph*, October 21, 1999.

"Understanding Colds." www.commoncold.org.

Underwood, Anne and Pat Wingert et al. "Stress in the Skies." *Newsweek*, November 29, 1999.

"Update on . . . chewing-gum." *The Independent*, February 11, 1997.

Vadentam, Shankar. "Do You Read Terms of Service Contracts?" NPR, August 23, 2016.

Veilleux, Zachary, "The 8 Worst Things You Can Do to Your Privates." *Men's Health*, November 1, 1998.

"Virus Attacks Cost Organizations $17.1 Billion in 2000." Computer Economics Press Release, January 5, 2001.

Von Radowitz, John. "Motoring: Why Road Rage and Murder Are Too Close for Comfort." *Birmingham Post*, January 5, 2001.

Waggoner, Susan. *Classic Household Hints*. New York: Stewart, Tabori & Chang, 2007.

Waldman, Katy. "The Psychology of Unfriending Someone on Facebook." *Slate*, April 24, 2014.

Ward, Robert. "Loud Music Stimulates Sex Center in the Brain." *The Daily Telegraph*, February 17, 2000.

———. "We All Scream After Ice Cream." *The Independent*, May 10, 1997.

Wardrop, Murray. "Women Are Better at Parking Than Men, Study Suggests." *The Telegraph*, January 29, 2012.

Wheeler, David R. "Voice Recognition Will Always Be Stupid." CNN, August 20, 2013.

Whitbourne, Susan Krauss. "Unfriended? Five Ways to Manage Online Rejection." *Psychology Today*. June 19, 2012.

Williams, Goeff. "9 Hidden Fees and How to Avoid Them." *U.S. News and World Report*, November 11, 2013.

Winans, Vanessa. "Can't Get It Out of My Head." *Toldeo Blade*, July 2, 2000.

———. "Itching To Know Why We Scratch." *Newsday*, July 30, 1996.

———. "Xmas Isn't a Plot to Take Christ out of Christmas." *Minneapolis Star Tribune*, December 21, 1997.

Wired. "Physicist Writes Mathematical Study to Avoid Traffic Ticket." April 16, 2012.

Wireless Flash News Service. "Chewing on Tinfoil Can Kill Germs." February 27, 1998.

Wolf, Anthony E. "Shut Your Mouth and Listen to Your Teens." *Globe and Mail*. November 24, 2011.

Worland, Justin. "Why Being Put on Hold Drives You Crazy." *Time*, March 31, 2015.

Wolchover, Natalie. "Science Reveals How Not to Spill Your Coffee While Walking." MSNBC. Updated May 9, 2012. http://www.msnbc.msn.com/id/47364282/ns/technology_and_science-science/t/science-reveals-how-not-spill-your-coffee-while-walking/.

Zhou, Li. "Can You Cure Chronic Lateness?" *The Atlantic*, June 2, 2016.